BIRMINGHAM
THE HIDDEN HISTORY

BIRMINGHAM
THE HIDDEN HISTORY

MICHAEL HODDER

In memory of my parents

First published in 2004 by Tempus Publishing

Reprinted with amendments in 2011 by
The History Press
The Mill, Brimscombe Port
Stroud, Gloucestershire GL5 2QG
www.thehistorypress.co.uk

British Library Cataloguing in Publication Data.
A catalogue record for this book is available from the British Library.

ISBN 978 0 7524 3135 2

Typesetting and origination by Tempus Publishing.
Printed and bound in Great Britain by
Marston Book Services Limited, Didcot

CONTENTS

ACKNOWLEDGEMENTS

This book includes results of the work of many individuals and organisations, whom I have specifically mentioned in the text as appropriate. I would particularly like to mention those who have inspired me and shared my enthusiasm for Birmingham's archaeology: the late Lawrence Barfield, Pete Bennett, Simon Buteux, Martin Cook, George Demidowicz, Toni Demidowicz, the late Margaret Gelling, Chris Hargreaves, Dawn Harris, John Hunt, Alex Jones, Terry Jones, Roger Lea, Peter Leather, Steve Litherland, Anthony Martin, Cathy Patrick (née Mould), Mike Nixon, Stephen Price, Stephanie Rátkai, the late Bert Round, Mike Shaw, Iain Soden, the late Mike Stokes, Dave Symons, Ruth Waller, Phil Watson and Sarah Watt.

I am extremely grateful to Lawrence Barfield, George Demidowicz, Toni Demidowicz, John Hunt, Alex Lang, Peter Leather, Steve Litherland, Cathy Mould, Stuart Palmer, Stephanie Ratkai, Dave Symons, Phil Watson and Sue Whitehouse for taking the time to read drafts of chapters and for making helpful suggestions which I am sure have improved the text.

The line drawings are by Shirley Ochi. Dave Symons assisted me with images from Birmingham Museums and Art Gallery. Neil Butler and Mike Shaw of Birmingham City Council produced and edited electronic versions of the photographs.

My late parents have always encouraged me and I dedicate this book in their memory.

Above all, Sue Whitehouse has shared and tolerated the disruption to our life that writing this book entailed, and is a constant source of support and encouragement.

This reprint is updated with information from archaeological work undertaken since early 2004.

CHAPTER 1

INTRODUCTION

Birmingham's recent history is associated with nationally and internationally famous characters like Mathew Boulton and Joseph Chamberlain, and a range of well-documented industries. The city's earlier history and even some aspects of its more recent development are under-appreciated. Sometimes the city is regarded as having no past before the eighteenth century, almost as though it had suddenly fallen out of the sky sometime during the industrial revolution and it has been assumed that, even if there was something happening in the area before this, few if any traces would have survived the intensive development of the last 300 years. However, cumulative archaeological information – particularly that derived from recent excavations as part of new development – has shown that nothing could be further from the truth. It has revealed the remains of thousands of years of the city's past, including many details from recent centuries.

This book is about what we know of Birmingham's past from archaeological sources: the physical remains left by its past inhabitants that show how they created, exploited and managed their environment. Many books and articles of varying length, scope and quality have been written about the history of Birmingham and the districts within it. With very few exceptions, most notably the recent book by Simon Buteux on the archaeological excavations in the Bull Ring, these have derived their information principally from documentary and topographic sources. This book brings together the archaeological evidence of the past of the whole city for the first time. It ranges in time from the earliest evidence for human activity in Birmingham in the Palaeolithic period or Old Stone Age up to the Cold War of the twentieth century. Much of this information, particularly that resulting from recent work, has not been published previously or has appeared in relatively inaccessible publications. In addition to bringing together information, the book reassesses some earlier interpretations of the archaeological evidence.

The area included in this book is the present-day city of Birmingham, extending from Sutton Coldfield in the north to Longbridge in the south *(1)*,

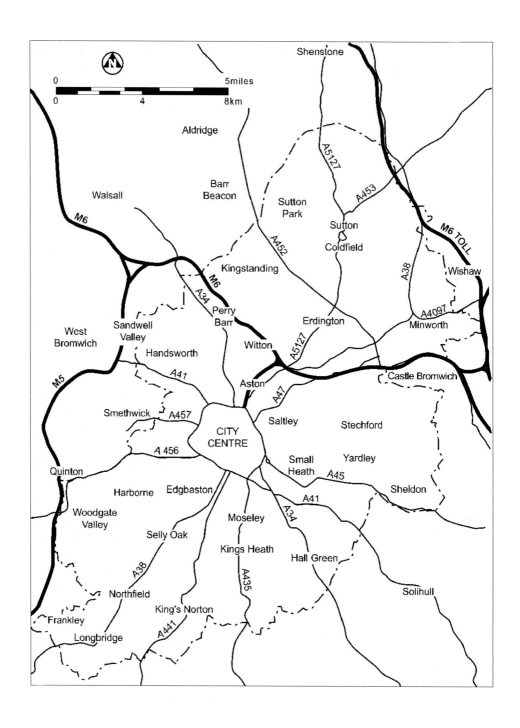

1 Main roads and localities. *Based on the Ordnance Survey map and reproduced by permission of Ordnance Survey on behalf of the Controller of Her Majesty's Stationery Office, © Crown Copyright 100042011*

but significant sites just outside the present city boundary are also included. It considers all types of archaeological evidence, defined as the human past represented by material remains, including man-made objects and structures surviving as below- or above-ground remains, together with associated evidence for the past environment. Although historic buildings are archaeological sites above ground, they are generally only included in this book if they have been studied using archaeological techniques.

THE PLACE: TOPOGRAPHY, GEOLOGY AND NATURAL RESOURCES

What opportunities did the city's topography and geology offer to its past inhabitants, and what restrictions did they pose? Birmingham lies in the English Midlands, just west of the centre of England. Much of the present-day city lies on the Birmingham Plateau, whose highest ground is on its southwestern, western, and north-western sides, rising to just over 200m above sea level within the present city boundaries. As the name suggests, it is a relatively flat area with few steep or abrupt slopes. Locally high points are separated by broad valleys with gently sloping sides. Birmingham's three rivers, the Rea, Cole and Tame, all drain to the north-east and east. None of them is navigable but in addition to providing water for domestic, agricultural and industrial use, their power and that of their tributary streams has been harnessed to drive water mills.

The geological formations underlying the city, the soils developing on them and therefore their agricultural capabilities and their potential use as a raw material, are simple if only the 'solid' geological formations are considered, but this is deceptive (2). To the south and east of a geological fault line across the city from Rubery in the south-west to Four Oaks in the north-east, passing through the city centre just east of St Martin's church and the Bull Ring, the geological solid is Mercia mudstone (formerly known as Keuper Marl). The city centre itself is on a ridge of Bromsgrove Sandstone (formerly known as Keuper Sandstone) running north-east to south-west, and to the west are Wildmoor Sandstones (formerly known as Bunter Sandstones) and Pebbly Sandstones of the Kidderminster Formation (formerly known as Bunter Pebble Beds), Hopwas Breccia and sandstone and conglomerate of the Salop Formation. The fault line could be regarded as a clear division between two quite different landscapes. The Mercia Mudstone is softer and more easily eroded than the sandstones, pebbly sandstones and conglomerates, although siltstones within it are more resistant to erosion and often form locally raised areas which have attracted settlement. It weathers to clay which can be used to make pottery, bricks and tiles and daub for walling. It is relatively impermeable, particularly when it has been compacted by animal trampling or cultivation, and is therefore poorly drained and tends to have much surface water.

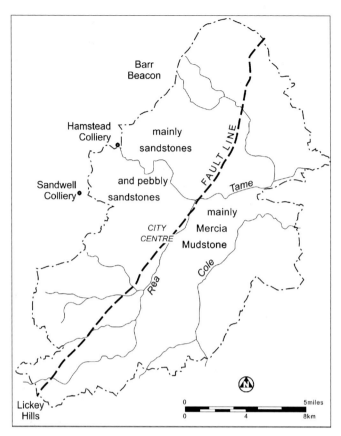

2 Rivers and broad geological division. *Based on the Ordnance Survey map and reproduced by permission of Ordnance Survey on behalf of the Controller of Her Majesty's Stationery Office, © Crown Copyright 100042011*

By way of compensation it is slightly calcareous and can therefore ameliorate soil acidity. In contrast, the sandstones and pebble beds are more resistant to erosion and give rise to sandy or sandy and pebbly soils respectively, which have less surface water but are loose and free draining and prone to drought, removal of nutrients through leaching, and erosion, particularly the pebbly soils. They provide sandstone for building and sand for casting.

Glacial drift covers much of Birmingham and the soils and topography resulting from it complicate this apparently straightforward twofold division. In some places clayey drift overlies sandstones, providing clay as a raw material (such as in Woodgate Valley in the south-west of the city) and resulting in more surface water and greater soil moisture retention. Drift overlying the Mercia Mudstone forms locally prominent ridges. Where it is sandy and pebbly these materials are available as a raw material and it results in well-drained soils. The extent and depth of drift explains the number of 'marl pits' in the part of the city on Mercia Mudstone. Some of these provided clay for bricks and tiles for construction of the buildings they adjoin, but the many on field edges or corners were dug to extract the underlying clay to improve the water retentiveness of the surface drift.

Modern perceptions of what this meant in terms of past land use are often based on current and recent soil conditions and agricultural practice, particularly mechanisation. These include the concept that clays were too heavy for ploughing before the introduction of suitable ploughs in the Middle Ages and that sandier soils were preferred. The observations of earlier writers are informative here; for example John Leland, who in his sixteenth-century description of his journey from Salford Bridge on the River Tame to Sutton Coldfield said that it was sandy ground – better for woods than for wheat.

Even Leland and others were writing after the impact of thousands of years of human activity which had directly or indirectly affected soil conditions through tree clearance and ploughing, causing erosion and leaching of nutrients, and through animal grazing preventing tree regeneration and compacting clay soils. The heathland of Sutton Park, developed on a free-draining sandy pebbly soil, is an artefact resulting from human management. In addition, individuals and communities had particular requirements for wood, timber and grazing land and met market demands for particular produce, and individuals controlled land use such as in the creation of deer parks in the medieval period.

Birmingham's natural resources are water, clay, sand, sandstone, pebbles and gravel as raw materials and water as a power source. No metal ore deposits or coal can be exploited from within the city boundary, although coal was mined under the city from Hamstead Colliery to the north-west. The smaller streams are frequently in substantial valleys containing peat deposits which have been exploited for domestic fuel. River terraces along the rivers and streams contain flint pebbles suitable for tool manufacture.

ARCHAEOLOGY AND THE HISTORY OF BIRMINGHAM

The archaeological evidence for Birmingham's past consists of surviving buildings, fragments of buildings or architectural details; earthworks, features visible on aerial photographs or historic maps, excavated remains, features detected by geophysical survey, objects found in field walking and chance finds. At a smaller scale but of no less importance, plant and animal remains and mineral residues provide direct evidence for the surrounding environment and agricultural and industrial processes. We can also infer how resources were exploited and managed from the archaeological evidence itself.

The available evidence reflects the city's current character and recent development and the type and location of archaeological work that has taken place. Birmingham is of course now predominantly covered by buildings and roads. The expansion of the city in the twentieth century, particularly between the First and Second World Wars and in the post-war period, resulted in Birmingham's historic town centre coalescing with the surrounding villages, hamlets and individual farms, and with the other historic town centre of Sutton Coldfield, making them suburbs. There is however still land in agricultural use on the north-eastern edge of the city, including arable and pasture, and some to its south. The non-agricultural open spaces consist of the heath, woods and grassland of Sutton Park, several country parks created from former agricultural land, and other suburban parks and open spaces.

Earlier archaeological work

Much of the archaeological information for Birmingham's past comes from research and fieldwork carried out relatively recently. For earlier generations of archaeologists, the absence of extensive areas of downland or moorland such as that in other parts of the country in which prehistoric and Roman remains survive as earthworks, a lack of perception of Birmingham as a historic town because it did not have Roman origins and had few surviving medieval buildings, the sparseness of its medieval documentation and a lack of appreciation of the significance of archaeological remains of more recent periods all conspired to discourage further enquiry. The benefit of this, however, is that most of our evidence is from archaeological work done to modern standards.

County histories written in the seventeenth century describe the most visible archaeological remains and mention discoveries of objects, such as the Roman road in Sutton Park which is mentioned in William Dugdale's *History and Antiquities of Warwickshire* (1656) and the Bronze Age palstave (a type of cast copper alloy axe) found in Handsworth which is described and illustrated in Robert Plot's *Natural History of Staffordshire* (1686). Local histories refer to chance finds and structures even though they might not be able to explain them, such as William Hutton's attribution of the earthworks of Metchley Roman fort to the Danes and the 'forgotten boundary' in Sutton Park mentioned and photographed by William Midgley in his *Sutton Coldfield Town and Chase* (1904). Perhaps the earliest record of structural remains revealed below ground was William Hutton's observation in 1775. He took down an old timber-framed house in High Street and noted that the foundation seemed to have been built mainly with stones from St Thomas's Priory, some of them apparently including architectural details. The earliest recorded archaeological excavation in Birmingham is that in 1859 of a mound in Sutton Park which was thought to be a prehistoric barrow or burial mound. Although Birmingham never benefited from the observations, drawings and descriptions of people like William Stukeley, its own antiquaries have provided invaluable information which has stimulated subsequent work. Christopher Chattock's *Antiquities* (1884) contains drawings and descriptions of earthworks, such as those on Hodge Hill Common, and records discoveries of objects, and G.B. Benton's article *Early Earthworks, Dykes and Hollow Roads of the Upland of Barr and Sutton Coldfield* (1906) contains, amongst much speculation, the earliest identification of the deer park earthworks in Sutton Park.

3 Excavations at Weoley Castle in 1938, showing the remains of a wooden bridge across the moat. *Copyright Birmingham Museums and Art Gallery*

During the first half of the twentieth century, some sites were explored by excavation, including the burnt mounds and Roman road in Sutton Park (1926 and 1936 respectively), Weoley Castle in the 1930s *(3)* and Metchley Roman fort (1934), the latter prompted by discoveries made during new development. The expansion of the city in the post-war period which included new residential development and the provision of more education facilities prompted state-funded 'rescue' excavations at Kent's Moat in Yardley (1959) and Metchley Roman fort (1967-69). The Kent's Moat excavation represents a relatively early national recognition of the importance of medieval archaeology. It accompanied locally-led research into Birmingham's moated sites which included salvage recording and small-scale excavation at Hawkesley Farm Moat in advance of and during residential development (1957-58), further excavation at Weoley Castle (1955-60), and excavation and earthwork recording at Gannow Green (1960s). A wider survey of areas likely to be developed in the south Birmingham area in the early 1970s included documentary research and building recording as well as earthwork survey and some excavation. Detailed recording of historic buildings in various parts of the city in the 1970s demonstrated the extent of survival and significance of this part of Birmingham's above-ground archaeology. In the north of the city, archaeological survey took place along the line of the A38 Sutton Coldfield bypass in 1970.

The range of Birmingham's archaeological remains was particularly demonstrated by two pieces of work on sites which are very nearly at opposite ends of the chronological spectrum. Michael Nixon's discoveries of prehistoric burnt mounds in south Birmingham in the 1950s and '60s through observation of stream banks was followed in 1980-81 by the excavation of the Cob Lane burnt mound, which was continued by further survey. This showed the importance of Birmingham's parks and open spaces for the survival of archaeological remains, and my own survey in Sutton Park in the 1970s recorded well-preserved earthworks of various dates. George Demidowicz's documentary research and field survey of watermills in the 1980s contributed to a greater awareness of industrial archaeology in the city as a whole and to excavation at Mathew Boulton's Soho Manufactory.

Finding Birmingham's archaeological remains

Earthworks are particularly well preserved in the city's parks and open spaces where there has been little or no disturbance other than natural weathering, but can also survive in residential areas such as the probable medieval estate boundary of New Hall in Sutton Coldfield which is visible in house gardens. Features are also visible in exposed stream banks, particularly prehistoric burnt mounds.

Geophysical survey has been used on burnt mounds, to trace the lines of Roman roads in current open spaces, and to locate post-medieval brick and tile kilns. Dendrochronology has provided dates for several timber-framed buildings and timber roofs of brick buildings. Most of the radiocarbon dates for archaeological sites in Birmingham are from burnt mounds. Beetles, seeds, pollen and soils from burnt mounds, Metchley Roman fort, the Roman road in Sutton Park, Gannow Green Moat and several medieval and post-medieval sites in the city centre have provided evidence about the past environment.

Field survey by fieldwalking, i.e. the systematic collection of objects from a ploughed field surface by walking at close intervals across it, formed part of the archaeological work along the line of the A38 in 1970. My own research in the Sutton Coldfield area in the 1980s, which included fieldwalking on specific types of site, was followed in the 1990s by an extensive archaeological survey by the Birmingham and Warwickshire Archaeological Society of the whole of the rural part of north-east Birmingham, primarily by fieldwalking (4). This has yielded prehistoric, Roman and medieval objects. Although there are obvious limitations in fieldwalking as a method of archaeological survey – it can only be undertaken on land which is currently in arable use, the visibility of objects depends on lighting and soil weathering, and the range of objects is limited mainly to pottery and flint or other stone – it does allow rapid coverage of large areas and enables identification of the concentrations of objects of particular periods across those areas.

4 Fieldwalking in Sutton Coldfield

'Chance finds' are objects which have been discovered during gardening, disturbance of ground for building, or walking on eroded surfaces in parks or open spaces, rather than in deliberate search. Such discoveries have been made throughout the city. The exact location of some of these is not precisely known; some objects that are described as being from 'near Birmingham' might actually have been found outside the city. Some are certainly, and others possibly, recent rather than ancient losses. Inevitably the range of objects found by chance is limited to those most easily recognised by non-archaeologists, and include coins – mainly Roman – and larger and more obvious stone and metal objects such as flint arrowheads and stone and metal axes. Despite these limitations, chance finds are particularly important as archaeological evidence from present residential areas and may indicate the presence of other features, such as the Roman pottery kiln in Sherifoot Lane, Sutton Coldfield, which was revealed by the chance discovery of pottery in 1987.

Most recent archaeological work in Birmingham has been necessitated by new development. The location and extent of the work is therefore deter-mined by the location of a development or proposed development and the cost is met by the developer. The first developer-funded excavation in Birmingham was at The Green in Kings Norton in 1992. There have subsequently been many excavations as part of new development in the city centre, notably from 1999 to 2001 as part of the redevelopment of the Bull Ring, and elsewhere in the city including extensive excavation at Metchley Roman fort. In the rural area, excavations in 2001 on the line of the M6 Toll motorway which clips the north-eastern edge of Birmingham revealed prehistoric and Roman remains. In addition, several historic buildings have been recorded in detail before renovation or alteration.

The city centre

The survival of archaeological remains in the city centre and their significance was not recognised until recently. Many people, even some archaeologists, thought that intensive development over the last few centuries would have destroyed whatever remained from earlier periods, and that archaeological remains of more recent times could not add to what we knew from documentary records. Recent large-scale excavations have dispelled this notion but even earlier small-scale work had shown that it was mistaken and misleading.

William Hutton's eighteenth-century discoveries have been described above. A sandstone wall thought to be part of the medieval Priory or Hospital of St Thomas was exposed in building work in 1898 *(5)*. Observations

5 Above Stone foundations of the Priory or Hospital of St Thomas, revealed in alterations to The Minories in April 1898. *Copyright Birmingham Museums and Art Gallery*

6 Opposite Excavations at Park Street in the city centre, with the Rotunda beyond. The large boundary ditch is on the left of the picture, under the brick wall

during the widening of High Street Deritend in 1953 revealed evidence for a medieval pottery industry, but no archaeological work at all took place before or during the construction of the Bull Ring Shopping Centre in the 1960s, although it included a large part of the medieval town centre. Birmingham lost out on the large state-funded excavations that took place in advance of the 1960s and '70s redevelopment because its medieval origins and significance were unappreciated, and the importance and archaeological remains of later date was not appreciated in the country as a whole. Between 1973 and 1975, during the redevelopment of the Wholesale Markets, remains of the medieval manor house, including part of a stone building, were recorded in far from ideal conditions, and there were small-scale excavations and observations in Deritend in the 1980s. In the 1990s excavations at the Old Crown, Hartwell Smithfield Garage and High Street Bordesley revealed below-ground remains of life and work in medieval and post-medieval Birmingham and on the other side of the city centre the below- and above-ground remains of the city's first gasworks were recorded. Between 1999 and 2001, excavations on Edgbaston Street, Moor Street, Park Street and part of the graveyard of St Martin's church in advance of the Bullring redevelopment revealed many details of life, work and death in the historic heart of Birmingham from the twelfth to the twentieth centuries *(6)*. Over the past few years the history of Birmingham's natural waterfront has been investigated in excavations near the River Rea at Gibb Street and Floodgate Street and remains of canal-side industries have been recorded. More remains of prehistoric Birmingham have been found, in Bournville, Northfield and even in the city centre.

The book is arranged in chronological order, with four chapters about specific time periods. A final chapter identifies some gaps in knowledge, picks out some themes that run through the book and looks at the protection and management of archaeological remains. An appendix lists and briefly describes some sites that can be visited.

CHAPTER 2
PREHISTORIC BIRMINGHAM

Thirty years ago an account of what we knew about prehistoric Birmingham would have been very short indeed and largely based on chance discoveries of objects such as flint arrowheads and stone and bronze axes, and antiquarian descriptions. Although chance discoveries are still an important source of information, we now have much more evidence *(7)*. Systematic searches of field surfaces in the rural area east of Sutton Coldfield have resulted in the discovery of Mesolithic and Neolithic flint tools and the debris from their manufacture. The discovery, dating and excavation of the mysterious burnt mounds, analysis of the data they provide on the ancient environment and reconstructions to explain their function have transformed our perceptions of Bronze Age Birmingham. Excavations along the line of the M6 Toll motorway in Sutton Coldfield have revealed Bronze Age and Iron Age sites and demonstrated not only how much survives but also how difficult it can be to locate. The information now available contradicts earlier preconceptions that the area was thinly populated in prehistoric times, which were based on the lack of prominent remains and lack of archaeological investigation.

HAND–AXES AND BIRMINGHAM'S FIRST INHABITANTS

In 1981 the occupier of a house in Court Lane, Erdington found a curiously shaped stone, 126mm (5in) long in his garden. It is one of the oldest man-made objects found in Birmingham – a Palaeolithic hand-axe made by chipping pieces off one end of a pebble to make a pointed tool that was held in the palm of the hand and used for cutting and chopping meat. The smoothed edges of the axe showed that it was not where its original owner had left or lost it, but that it had been moved in gravels by glacial melt water.

A similar hand-axe *(8)* was found in 1890 following observations over a long period in the gravels of the River Rea at Saltley, presumably inspired by discoveries of Palaeolithic objects in quarries in southern England. The

Loaches Banks
Manorial Wood
Hillwood Common Road
Sutton Park
Collets Brook
Langley Mill Farm
Langley Brook
Kings Standing
Wishaw Hall Farm
Court Lane
Peddimore
Sandwell Priory
Witton Hall
Berwood
CITY CENTRE
Saltley
Manor House
Brook Lane
Metchley
Fox Hollies Park
Yachting Pool
Moseley Bog
Cob Lane
Police Station
Woodlands Park
Berry Mound

| 0 | | | 5miles |
| 0 | 4 | | 8km |

7 *Above* Prehistoric sites mentioned in the text (find spots of individual objects are not shown). *Based on the Ordnance Survey map and reproduced by permission of Ordnance Survey on behalf of the Controller of Her Majesty's Stationery Office, © Crown Copyright 100042011*

8 *Right* Palaeolithic hand-axe from Saltley. *Copyright Birmingham Museums and Art Gallery*

gravels overlay Mercia Mudstone and were exposed near Saltley College in a pit dug to extract clay for brick-making. The hand-axe was made from a brown quartzite pebble and is about 100mm (4in) long. John Evans describes this find in his book *The Ancient Stone Implements, Weapons and Ornaments of Great Britain* (1897) and asks

> …whether the assumed absence of Palaeolithic implements over this area may not be due to their not having been found, and not to their non-existence…

The Saltley axe shows that gravel deposits containing paleolithic objects do survive in Birmingham, as does the reputed discovery of another axe in the side of a quarry in Brook Road in Edgbaston, near the Chad Brook, a tributary stream of the River Rea. These axes were probably made and used nearly half a million years ago. Another handaxe of slightly later type has been found in Sutton Coldfield.

In the 1950s and '60s boreholes and earthmoving as part of new development in Nechells, Duddeston and Washwood Heath (north of Saltley) revealed silt and peat containing pollen, seeds and beetles which indicate what the landscape was like about 400,000 years ago. This was an interglacial period when the temperature rose and glacial melt water moved the gravel containing the hand-axes. Pollen and seeds show that as the climate became warmer, pine and birch were replaced by oak, ash and alder. The beetle species from the warmer period were like those inhabiting Britain now, suggesting that climatic conditions were little different from today. As colder conditions returned, and the country headed toward glaciation once more, pine dominated again. Deposits of the same period were also exposed in Quinton, in ground investigations preceding the construction of the M5 motorway.

A layer of peat which was exposed during construction of the Wholesale Markets near the medieval manor house site in the city centre (described in Chapter 4) shows what Birmingham's climate was like in more recent times. It contained insect species found nowadays in more mountainous regions of Britain and in northern Scandinavia or Russia, indicating the colder conditions of the last glacial period, about 11,000 years ago. Our next evidence for people in Birmingham is from shortly after that, when conditions were warmer. It again consists of stone tools.

FROM HUNTERS TO FARMERS:
MESOLITHIC, NEOLITHIC AND INTO THE BRONZE AGE

The Palaeolithic hand-axes were made from rounded quartzite pebbles – the type of stone you can find in most Birmingham gardens, fields or stream beds. The flint nodules used to make similar tools in other parts of the country do not occur in the Birmingham area, but there are smaller flint pebbles in some of the glacial drift which covers large parts of the city and in the gravel terraces of Birmingham's rivers. Birmingham's inhabitants in the Mesolithic period used these flint pebbles as a raw material for their tools and weapons. Their successors, Birmingham's first farmers, supplemented this resource with tools made from better-quality flint mined in southern or eastern England and acquired axes made of other types of stone, by trade or gift, from various parts of the country.

The base of a soil layer surviving in natural hollows near Banbury Street in the city centre was dated to about 8000 BC, in the early Mesolithic period. It contained two worked flints and pollen in it showed that at this time the site lay in pine and birch woodland. The flint tools and waste flakes used by people gathering wild food plants, fishing and hunting in Birmingham in the later part of the Mesolithic period (between about 6000 and 4000 BC) have generally been found close to streams, such as the 12 pieces of worked flint, including two scrapers, blades and flakes, which were found from near Little Bracebridge Pool in Sutton Park. Although the pool itself was constructed in the medieval period, the stream feeding it and its surrounding wetlands would have been attractive to hunters and gatherers for the plant and animal resources it offered. Other Mesolithic flint has been found by fieldwalking, such as at Manorial Wood, also in Sutton Coldfield. These small quantities may represent no more than the tools of a hunting party or an overnight campsite, but larger quantities of worked flints from this period have been found just outside Birmingham. At Bourne Pool near Loaches Banks over 2,000 pieces were found next to a stream by fieldwalking, in an excavation at Wishaw Hall Farm over 1,400 late Mesolithic worked flints were found on a slope overlooking a stream, and in excavations on the Sandwell Priory site in Sandwell Valley over 800 flints were found near a spring and many stake-holes may be the remains of temporary houses or shelters from this time. These sites are currently dated by the type of flint tools and debris found on them.

A few polished stone axes of the Neolithic period (about 4000–2500 BC) have been found in Birmingham. These were chance discoveries, with the exception of the axe found by Robert Sherlock in his observations during the widening of High Street Deritend in 1953, 2ft (60cm) below the present ground surface. The Deritend axe and axes found on the Minworth Sewage Works and in Northfield are made of stone from Langdale in the Lake District. Other stone axes found in Birmingham are made of stone from Leicestershire, North Wales and Cornwall and from flint from eastern or southern England. The widespread sources indicate trading links across the country at this time. Assuming that these axes were actually used as tools, rather than having a symbolic value, they were presumably for felling trees to clear land for agriculture and to cut wood for building and for firewood. Flint arrowheads have also been found in various parts of Birmingham. Stone axes and flint arrowheads have been discovered by chance during gardening or ground disturbance for building, but less distinctively shaped tools and the debris from flint tool manufacture are only likely to be noticed during deliberate search through excavation or fieldwalking. The majority of flint tools and debris from flint tool manufacture found in systematic fieldwalking at several locations in the rural area in Sutton Coldfield north-east of Birmingham is probably Neolithic in date, although Mesolithic material is also present. The Neolithic flint tools from here are all scrapers, including one which has been reshaped as a knife, and the manufacturing debris consists of flakes and the cores from which they have been struck. The concentrations of worked flint probably indicate the location of settlements, which may have been occupied seasonally rather than permanently.

The oldest man-made structures that we can identify in Birmingham as yet belong to the Neolithic or early Bronze Age periods. A small pit exposed by a trench for a new sewer pipe near Bournville Lane and dated to about 2700 BC contained 28 pieces of late Neolithic pottery from tub or bucket-shaped vessels called 'Grooved Ware' from their distinctive decoration. Pollen preserved in a layer of peat near the River Tame in Perry Barr dating from around the same time showed that the landscape there was mainly woodland consisting of lime, oak, Scots pine, alder and hazel trees. An aerial photograph shows what may be a Neolithic 'cursus' monument near Hillwood Common Road. The mound which gives its name to the modern suburb of Kingstanding is probably a prehistoric barrow or burial mound of the later Neolithic or early Bronze Age (up to about 1700 BC) (9). It is in a prominent position overlooking Sutton Park to the north and Birmingham city centre to the south. The mound is about 20m in diameter and about 1m high. There are slight traces of a ditch around the base of the mound, from which earth to construct it would have been dug. The mound is said to get its name from the fact that King Charles I stood on it to review his troops during the civil war, and it was even suggested that it was actually built then, but its name occurs in documents before Charles's time. The name may be related to its use or even construction as a hunting stand for observation of game in the medieval period, when the area in which it lies was heathland within Sutton Chase. The heath was brought into agricultural use at the beginning of the nineteenth century when, according to G.B. Benton writing in 1906, 'a considerable treasure of silver chains' was found, although he does not specify whether or not it was found in the mound. Benton also says he was told that the mound was destroyed when the ground around it was cleared and that the mound was subsequently reconstructed.

Recent fieldwork has shown that two other mounds in Birmingham are not prehistoric barrows as previously thought. In his book *Antiquities* (1884), Christopher Chattock included a description and plan of a group of mounds on Hodge Hill Common which he said consisted of one large oval mound, three circular mounds and one rectangular mound. Observations by Dawn Harris exactly 100 years later showed that Chattock's large oval mound is defined by a bank and ditch which overlie and are therefore later than ridge and furrow.

9 Kingstanding Mound. The ditch is visible at the base of the mound, on the left

The date of the ridge and furrow is not known but it is unlikely to be older than the Middle Ages. The oval mound may be an artificial rabbit warren, and the rectangular mound, which is alongside a road, is more likely to be the site of a building. It could have been a dwelling erected as part of encroachment on common land in the Middle Ages or later, as described in chapter 4.

It was also suggested that a mound near Longmoor Pool in Sutton Park was a barrow and this interpretation was given some support when a trench and pits dug across it in 1859 revealed that the first 3ft of soil were 'artificial, of disturbed soil'. However, excavations by the University of Birmingham in 2001 showed that the mound was a natural hill, but that there were archaeological remains on it which probably related to more recent military training. These are discussed in Chapter 5.

There may well be other barrows in Birmingham whose mounds no longer survive but whose surrounding ditches may be detected in excavation, but two 'ring ditches' found near Langley Brook just outside the city boundary in excavations along the line of the M6 Toll motorway proved to be Iron Age houses rather than Bronze Age barrows. One of them consisted of a ditch forming a ring about 12m in diameter.

BIRMINGHAM'S BRONZE AGE:
BARROWS, STONE HAMMERS AND BRONZE AXES

The barrows bring us into the Bronze Age (about 2500 to 700 BC) but archaeological evidence from elsewhere in the country shows that the technological innovations indicated in the period's name were not reflected in its earlier part by changes in settlement patterns or economy. Indeed, stone tools were still in use, including those made from flint and tools of other stones that have a hole drilled into them to hold a haft. These include rounded 'mace heads' or 'pebble hammers' from Perry Common and Barr Beacon, possibly symbols of office as the first name implies, and 'axe-hammers' with a blade at one end and a flat face on the other, found at Kings Norton and Stirchley.

Like these four objects, the small quantity and narrow range of cast bronze artefacts found in Birmingham were all found by chance. Part of a poorly-cast early Bronze Age flat axe was found in Sutton Park. Palstaves, cast axes dating to the middle of the Bronze Age which were shaped with recesses to hold a wooden haft securely, have been found in Handsworth (the one mentioned by Robert Plot in 1686), Kings Heath and Stechford. The middle Bronze Age palstaves are contemporary with the numerous burnt mounds described below. A bronze axe from Hall Green, with a socket to house its haft, is late Bronze Age in date.

Other than burnt mounds, the only definite Bronze Age feature so far found in Birmingham is a pit in Northfield (see below). A possible timber structure, consisting of worked timbers forming a platform or trackway across peat in Sutton Park is recorded in an antiquarian account. 'Incola', writing in 1762, describes the discovery during peat-cutting of

> ... thousands of fir trees, cut down by the Romans, to enable them to pass over
> a morass there. The bodies of the trees are sometimes dug up sound, with the
> marks of the axe upon them.

He thought that the trees were a trackway from the nearby Roman road, but his description is more suggestive of a prehistoric trackway like those found in various wetlands in Britain and Ireland which range in date from the Neolithic to the Iron Age.

A site near Langley Brook in Sutton Coldfield, originally detected on an aerial photograph and subsequently excavated in advance of construction of the M6 Toll motorway, has been dated to about 100 BC and is therefore contemporary with the Iron Age enclosure to its north-west, described below (p. 48). It consisted of a ditch surrounding a rhomboid area about 30m across, containing a single curving gully about 6m across, probably a drainage trench around a circular timber house *(10)*. There were west and east-facing entrance gaps in the ditch, the latter of which was later blocked. Construction of the Northfield Relief Road revealed a small pit filled with clay, charcoal and ash. Radiocarbon dating of the charcoal showed that the pit dated to about 1600 BC, in the Bronze Age. This overlaps with the earliest dates for Birmingham's burnt mounds.

BURNT MOUNDS: NEW LIGHT ON BRONZE AGE BIRMINGHAM

Heat-shattered stones *(11)* are the main component of burnt mounds, the most numerous type of prehistoric site known in Birmingham and its immediate surroundings. Nearly 40 burnt mounds have been found in Birmingham. They consist of mounds 10–20m across composed of heat-shattered pebbles and charcoal. They are normally found near streams and are often discovered as a layer of heat-shattered stones and charcoal in a stream bank. A few sites are still visible as actual mounds, and others are represented by concentrations of heat-shattered stones on ploughed field surfaces.

Burnt mounds are not confined to Birmingham but have been found in large numbers throughout Britain and Ireland (where they are known as *fulachta fianna* or *fiadha*). Where the mounds survive well, particularly in Ireland and the Northern Isles, they are horseshoe-, crescent- or kidney-shaped, up to 20m across and 1m high, and enclose a stone or timber-lined trough. The sites are usually next to streams or other sources of water, often in wet locations that are not ideal for settlement. Excavations of burnt mounds have revealed stone and timber structures, including buildings and hearths. Radiocarbon dates place most of the sites in the range 2000–800 BC. Excavation of burnt mounds characteristically yields few or no objects. Animal bone is relatively rare.

Several processes using heated stones ('hot stone technology') could have resulted in the formation of burnt mounds. These include cooking food in water boiled with hot stones, sauna-type bathing in steam produced by pouring water on hot stones, or industries using steam or hot water such as dyeing or felting cloth, leatherworking or woodworking. The sheer quantity of burnt mounds in some parts of Britain and Ireland and their unglamorous nature (they have been described as 'one of the most boring sites with which a field archaeologist must deal'!) has led to some disregard of the sites,

10 Prehistoric enclosure near Langley Brook, downstream from a burnt mound. The corner of the infilled enclosure ditch is visible as a light band

11 Heat-shattered pebbles in a burnt mound at Moseley Bog

but because they are so numerous they must be telling us something about the wider landscapes to which they belong. In addition, waterlogged layers adjoining the mounds contain data on past environmental conditions.

Birmingham's burnt mounds have been investigated by observation of stream banks, field survey, geophysical survey and excavation. They are particularly conducive to survey by geophysical techniques: to resistance survey because the burnt stone mounds themselves are free-draining in contrast to the wet areas in which they normally lie, and to magnetic survey because the stones have been heated. Geophysical survey and excavation have demonstrated the complexity of these apparently simple sites. Radiocarbon dates for Birmingham's burnt mounds have been obtained from charcoal from excavated burnt mounds and charcoal samples from mounds exposed in stream banks. Reconstructions have been undertaken to test the interpretation of the sites. The number of burnt mounds implies a far greater population in the Birmingham area in this period than was previously thought. The discovery and investigation of Birmingham's burnt mounds and subsequent alternative interpretations has stimulated a wider awareness about these sites in Britain, Ireland and beyond.

The first burnt mounds to be discovered in the Birmingham area were those at Aldridge, Pelsall and Middleton, in the early part of the twentieth century. The majority have subsequently been found through deliberate search of stream banks and in fieldwalking. Other sites have been identified from references in antiquarian accounts, such as that of William Fowler, who says in his *History of Erdington* (1885) that about 50 years previously his father had noticed several large, turf-covered mounds in one of the meadows at Berwood, which were shown to contain large heaps of broken stones and were subsequently used to repair farm roads. The content of these mounds and their location near the River Tame or one of its tributary streams suggest that they were burnt mounds. The burnt mound at Middleton, just outside Birmingham, was also removed for road repairs, and the markedly level rather than rounded surface of the burnt mound excavated at Cob Lane, described below, suggested that part of it had been removed to provide stone for the adjacent Bristol Road. The heat-cracked stones could easily be broken up into small fragments which could then be compacted into a road surface.

The first archaeological excavation of burnt mounds in Birmingham was in Sutton Park. A fire in about 1900 exposed a low pear-shaped mound with a hollow on the top of it. A subsequent severe fire in 1921 revealed a total of six mounds arranged in an arc and exposed patches of heat-shattered stones within them *(12)*. Small-scale excavation by W.L. Bullows in 1926 consisted of trenches across the mounds and showed that they were all composed of heat-shattered stones and that hollows in the tops of the two largest mounds, both pear-shaped, corresponded to pits under them. Uneven ground to the east of the mounds was interpreted as the site of a contemporary settlement

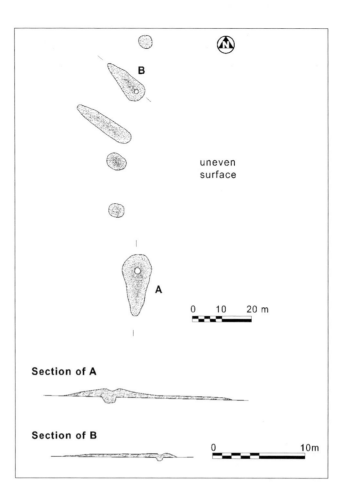

uneven surface

0 10 20 m

B

A

12 *Right* Sutton Park burnt mounds. *From a plan by W.L. Bullows*

13 *Below* The burnt mound at the Yachting Pool in Bournville, visible in the stream bank as a mass of heat-shattered pebbles and charcoal

Section of A

Section of B

0   10m

14 Excavation of the burnt mound at Cob Lane

site and a possible hut circle was identified within it. No objects were found, and the excavation took place about 20 years before radiocarbon dating was developed, so the mounds could not be dated by this method. The Sutton Park burnt mounds are unusual in their location, in that they are at some distance from a stream, but they are similar in size and form to the burnt mounds recorded elsewhere in the Birmingham area.

In the 1950s and '60s, Michael Nixon discovered 11 burnt mounds in south Birmingham, most of which were visible as layers of heat-shattered stones and charcoal in stream banks. In 1970 a sample of charcoal from the Yachting Pool site in Bournville *(13)*, one of those discovered by Nixon, was radiocarbon dated to about 1200 BC, demonstrating its Bronze Age date. All but one of the radiocarbon dates that have since been obtained for burnt mounds in Birmingham and the surrounding area lie between 1700 and 1000 BC.

The burnt mound at Cob Lane

The most thoroughly investigated burnt mound in Birmingham so far is that at Cob Lane on Griffins Brook in south Birmingham, which was discovered by Michael Nixon in 1950 and excavated by Lawrence Barfield and myself in 1980 and 1981 *(14)*. In addition to providing information on the burnt mound itself, the sequence of layers and the plant and animal remains contained in them revealed what this part of south Birmingham looked like just over 3,000 years ago. They demonstrated the impact of people on that environment, including evidence for forest clearance, woodland management, cultivation and grazing animals, and possibly metalworking, and contributed to the interpretation of the function of these sites.

The burnt mound itself was up to 9m across and up to 0.50m (1ft 8in) high *(15)*. It contained an estimated 8 tonnes of heat-shattered quartzite pebbles. The charcoal in the burnt mound itself was from young stem or branch wood, probably off-cuts from coppiced trees. It was predominantly alder, together with alder buckthorn and willow, which could all have grown alongside the stream. Of these, alder makes a better fuel when used as charcoal than as wood and was probably coppiced for this purpose. It is unlikely that charcoal was made as a fuel for the burnt mound, but it could have been made for metalworking and the surplus used in the burnt mound. The quartzite pebbles used in the burnt mound would have been obtainable from the bed of the stream adjoining the site. A radiocarbon date of about 1400 BC was obtained for wood from the lower levels of the mound. Although all the soil, charcoal and stone excavated at Cob Lane was sieved because of the small number of objects found in excavations at other burnt mounds, only two animal bones and a worked flint were found on the whole site, and the only one of these from the mound of heat-shattered stone itself was a burnt cow tooth.

The mound was originally within a stream meander, and the former bed of the stream was found to its north-east and south-west. Various features below

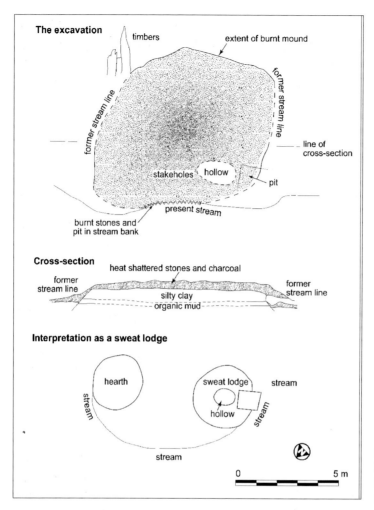

The excavation

timbers

extent of burnt mound

former stream line

former stream line

line of cross-section

stakeholes   hollow

pit

present stream

burnt stones and pit in stream bank

Cross-section

heat shattered stones and charcoal

former stream line

former stream line

silty clay

organic mud

Interpretation as a sweat lodge

hearth

sweat lodge   stream

stream

hollow

stream

stream

0   5 m

15 Plan and cross-section of Cob Lane burnt mound, and interpretation of it as a sweat lodge

the mound were related to its use but had been covered by heat-shattered stones and charcoal after the site had been abandoned. A pit about a metre square and 0.40m (1ft 4in) deep, on the former stream bank that formed the edge of the mound, had traces of a wooden lining and two successive clay bases. It was probably originally separated from the stream bank by a sluice, perhaps a moveable plank. Next to the square pit, opposite the former stream bank, there was a shallow oval hollow about 2m long and 1m wide whose surface was reddened by heat *(16)*. A second pit was visible in the present stream bank. Based on the usual interpretation of burnt mounds and features found at burnt mounds in other parts of the British Isles as the remains of a cooking process, we initially interpreted the hollow as the hearth where the stones were heated and the pit as a container of water into which hot stones were placed, but this interpretation was changed as a result of the experimental reconstructions of burnt mounds as described below. There were also several holes resulting from pointed wooden stakes being pressed into the surface of the clayey silt under the mound.

16 The pit and reddened hollow on the edge of the former stream channel at the Cob Lane burnt mound. The heat-shattered stones and charcoal of the mound are visible on the edge of the excavation

The story revealed by the excavation at Cob Lane actually starts before, although not long before, the burnt mound accumulated. The burnt mound lay on a dome of orange silty clay up to 60cm (2ft) thick, which in turn lay on top of a layer of mud containing tree trunks, branches and large numbers of hazel nut shells and beetle remains. A radiocarbon date of about 1370 BC was obtained from hazelnut shells from the mud layer. Two large oak tree trunks on the edge of the original stream bank may have been washed out from the organic mud into the stream but could have been deliberately placed there by the users of the site to prevent the burnt stones and charcoal slipping into the stream that surrounded it. Despite this, dumps of burnt stones and charcoal had been tipped or slipped down the bank over the tree trunks during the life of the mound.

The radiocarbon dates for the mud layer under the mound and the mound itself are virtually identical, showing that little time separated them. The environment of Bronze Age south Birmingham indicated by the waterlogged wood, hazelnut shells, beetle remains and caddis larvae in the mud is therefore likely to be same as that of the burnt mound. All the beetle species are still found in Britain and show that the climate of Bronze Age Birmingham was similar to that of today. The beetle species and the caddis larvae showed that Griffins Brook at this time was a small, rapidly flowing stream over a stony or gravel bed running through woodland and shaded by overhanging trees which included alder and hazel, surviving as waterlogged wood in the mud layer. The stream would wash away rather than retain sediments which accumulated slowly, so the mud and the clayey silt over it must have been rapidly washed into the stream valley. The quantity of hazelnut shells shows that the woodland was not dense, and the beetles show that the woodland was open enough to permit the growth of a ground layer of herbs and shrubs. There were also beetles that live in the dung of grazing animals, suggesting some grassland, together with a species that feeds on lime trees.

The mud and the clayey silt above it also tell us how people were drastically affecting their environment shortly before the burnt mound was established. The mud may result from clearance of forest which contained oak trees, represented by the tree trunks, and lime, represented by the beetle species that feed on it. The clayey silt above this is likely to be soil which had been loosened by ploughing on the slopes above the site, following clearance of trees, and washed down towards the stream by greater run-off resulting from forest clearance. The quantity of material washed down and the hazel nuts in the mud layer suggest that the ploughing took place in the late autumn for winter-sown cereals.

This sequence of layers and the activities it implies is not restricted to the Cob Lane site but has also been observed at two nearby burnt mounds. At the police station site, less than 100m downstream from Cob Lane, a burnt mound exposed in a sewer pipe trench overlay a silty clay, like that at Cob Lane, under which there was an organic mud containing wood and oak tree trunks. The sequence of tree ring widths in the oak trunks possibly matched the sequence of tree rings in Ireland for the period between 1300 BC and 1200 BC, but unfortunately a definite match could not be obtained. The burnt mound exposed in the bank of Griffins Brook at the Yachting Pool about 500m downstream from Cob Lane also overlies orange silty clay.

The extent of burnt mounds

The Cob Lane excavation was followed by a systematic search of stream banks in south Birmingham to locate other sites, continuing the work begun by Michael Nixon. Twenty burnt mounds were found along the 35km (22 miles) of stream searched. This type of search is of course only possible where the stream banks are exposed, not where the banks are revetted or the stream itself culverted underground, so there may be many more sites which are not visible. In the Sutton Coldfield area, additional sites have been discovered as concentrations of heat-shattered stones on field surfaces as well as in stream banks. Other sites have been found through observation of soil stripping for construction near the Roman fort at Metchley in south Birmingham, and on the line of the M6 Toll motorway in Sutton Coldfield.

Discoveries so far suggest that burnt mounds are fairly evenly distributed throughout the Birmingham area. They have shown that burnt mounds occur in close proximity to each other, in clusters and in pairs, usually of two sites of different size.

On the Coldbath Brook in Moseley Bog, the main mound, which is visible as a low mound with a stream running through it, is approximately circular and is about 13m in diameter. A second burnt mound is about 11m east of the first and is visible as a layer of heat-shattered stones 3.3m long and up to 4cm (about 1½in) thick in the north bank of the stream. The larger of the two burnt mounds on the Gallows Brook in Woodlands Park is oval, about 11m long and at least 6m wide. The smaller site, just 70m upstream, is visible as a layer of burnt pebbles 3m long and only about 0.20m (8in) thick. Alex Jones's excavations at Metchley, along a 75m length of a former stream course, revealed two or three burnt mounds and other features including probable hearths and pits containing heat-shattered stones *(17)*.

The burnt mound on the Westley Brook in Fox Hollies Park survives as a mound 14m long and 9m wide. Unusually for Birmingham burnt mounds, it is shaped like a horseshoe, with the opening to the north. There is a short raised bank about 10m long to its east. A resistance survey by Alex Jones on and around the visible mound revealed other features extending up to 60m from the mound, including arcs of burnt stones, probable pits and hearths and former stream channels *(18)*. On the line of the M6 Toll motorway in Sutton Coldfield, two sites were found on adjacent streams, Langley Brook and Collets Brook, about 800m (0.5 mile) apart.

Downstream from the burnt mound on the Langley Brook, which was characteristically composed of fragmented burnt stone and charcoal, shallow natural hollows contained burnt stone only, interleaved with alluvium. Such areas of relatively large heat-shattered stones without charcoal, in contrast to the mixture of fragments of heat-shattered stone and charcoal which normally occur in burnt mounds, may be stones washed from a burnt mound further upstream or may relate to the use of the sites. Heat-shattered stones alone or mixed with charcoal have also been found in features other than burnt mounds such as ring-ditches of Iron Age date and Roman enclosure ditches on the M6 Toll motorway and in a pit at the Roman farmstead in Longdales Road in Kings Norton.

The use of burnt mounds

The explanation of burnt mounds as cooking sites is derived from early Irish literature which describes the use of heated stones to boil water in which meat was cooked, and the heat-shattered stones and even burnt mounds themselves are often called 'pot boilers' from this interpretation. Many experiments and reconstructions have shown that a joint of meat can be cooked in this way and that the debris resulting from the process consists of shattered stones and charcoal, like that in burnt mounds. It is an uncomfortable and inefficient method of cooking a joint of meat, but little thought seems to have been

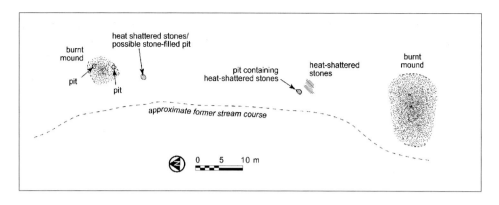

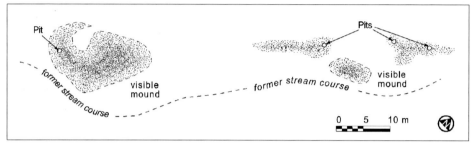

17 Top Metchley burnt mounds. *Redrawn from plans by Alex Jones*

18 Above Fox Hollies burnt mounds. *Redrawn from plans by Alex Jones*

given to this. If burnt mounds were used for cooking we might expect to find animal bones and other debris in them. At some sites the absence of bone could be explained by an acid soil, but this is not the case at Cob Lane and other Birmingham sites. When we found no evidence for food preparation, cooking or consumption at the Cob Lane burnt mound, Lawrence Barfield and I suggested, flippantly at first, that heated stones might have been used to produce steam for sweat or sauna-type bathing. Another argument in favour of this interpretation is the location of burnt mounds in wet areas prone to flooding and therefore not conducive to settlement, but where there was access to water that could have been used as a cold plunge. This explanation had previously been put forward in 1965 by the Irish archaeologist A.T. Lucas and we revived it by research into the archaeological and ethnographic evidence which demonstrated the long history, wide distribution and varied techniques of sweat bathing. This showed that sweat bathing was the most efficient method of personal hygiene, especially in cold latitudes, before the development of tub bathing and modern plumbing, that sweat or steam bathing using hot stones was widespread in the Old and the New Worlds, and that sweat bathing had, and still has, important ritual overtones, which combined the idea of purification, both spiritual and physical.

Inevitably not all archaeologists agree with this interpretation but at least it stimulated more discussion and appreciation of burnt mounds which had up to then been rather neglected. A range of other uses of 'hot stone technology' which might result in burnt mounds has been suggested, including cloth fulling, dyeing and felting, leatherworking and woodworking. We should not assume, however, that all burnt mounds had the same function and indeed where there are two or more burnt mounds close to each other they may have been used for different purposes.

Several physical reconstructions have taken place to test the interpretation of burnt mounds as sweat lodges. These are based on the excavated evidence from Cob Lane and on the contemporary and traditional sweat lodges of North American Indians in which steam is produced by pouring water on hot stones placed in a shallow hollow inside a tent made of animal hides on a framework of bent-over branches. The first of these reconstructions took place in June 1998 and was prompted by a visit to the burnt mound site at Moseley Bog in Birmingham by a modern 'New Age' sweat lodge user, Mark Graham. As far as I am aware this was the first time that a reconstruction based on the sweat lodge interpretation had been carried out.

The reconstructions have replicated the archaeological evidence and have therefore demonstrated the validity of the interpretation of burnt mounds as steam baths or saunas but this does not of course invalidate other interpretations. The reconstructions show that, used in steam bathing, burnt mounds have at least two elements; the hearth and the sweat lodge with its hollow and water sump, and possibly a third; the area where burnt stone used in the sweat lodge was discarded. The mound of fragmented heat-shattered stones and charcoal, the actual 'burnt mound', represents the location of the fire on which the stones were heated. The sweat lodge structure could be as much as 10m from the mound, and might well be indicated by the smaller sites in apparently paired examples or by areas of larger heat-shattered stones without charcoal. This would explain the range and extent of features at burnt mound sites such as Fox Hollies Park and the occurrence of burnt mounds in pairs, which could represent two parts of the same process or two different uses of hot stone technology on the same site.

All of the reconstructions have followed the same basic layout, in which the sweat lodge is about 6m away from the fire on which the stones were heated (*19* and *20*). This layout is consistent with the excavated evidence from Cob Lane, where the sweat lodge would have been at one end of the stream meander occupied by the burnt mound, and the hearth at the other *(15)*.

Rounded pebbles were cleaned and heated on a wood fire using brash cut from coppice. The size of the brash is consistent with the size of the charcoal found in the Cob Lane burnt mound. Much charcoal was left in the base of the fire because of the reducing conditions created here. Heating caused the stones to crack but they did not break up until they were moved, which resulted in

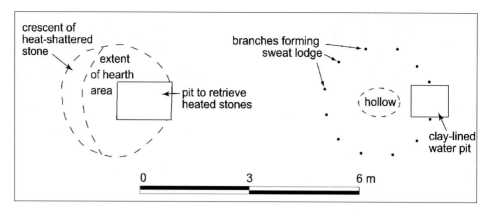

19 Plan of a sweat lodge reconstruction

the distinctive jagged breaks like those in stones in burnt mounds. A pit in front of the hearth, replicating pits or troughs at burnt mounds, might have served to help retrieve heated stones from the fire and could have held a container to carry hot stones from the hearth to the sweat lodge. The framework of the sweat lodge was constructed of pliable poles cut from coppice. Their pointed ends were inserted in holes on a circle about 3m in diameter and bent over to form a domed structure *(21)*. Repeated re-erection of such a structure would result in the mass of stakeholes found on excavated burnt mound sites. In the reconstruction the framework was covered with tarpaulins to replicate animal hides. A sod about 40cm (1ft 4in) across was removed from the centre of the structure to create a shallow hollow. Heated stones were taken from the fire and placed in the hollow. Antler was found be a suitable tool for this. Fragments of stone too small to pick up were left in the fire amongst ash and charcoal.

A pit was dug on the edge of, and protruding into, the sweat lodge, and was lined with clay to hold water. Water was scooped from this onto the stones in the hollow to produce steam. This arrangement replicates the stream–side pit at Cob Lane and the adjoining fire-reddened hollow in the subsoil, now inter-preted as the hollow into which the hot stones were placed to be dowsed with water to produce steam. The exposed subsoil in the hollow would have been scorched by the heat of the stones and continued removal of hot stones would have enlarged the hollow and smoothed its sides. The stones could then be discarded anywhere, but at least some of them would still be large enough to be reheated and used again, and therefore would be taken back to the fire site.

The hearth debris consists of heat shattered stone fragments which were too small to remove, and unused heated stones, together with charcoal and ash, just like that found in burnt mounds. When the hearth area is cleared for a subsequent fire, the debris also tends to be naturally scraped into a crescent, the characteristic shape of burnt mounds. The mix of fragmented heat-shattered

20 Sweat lodge reconstruction based on the excavated evidence from Cob Lane. The stones are heated on the fire in the foreground and taken in the sweat lodge beyond. The stream would have flowed behind and to the right of the sweat lodge and the hearth

21 The framework of the reconstructed sweat lodge, with the hollow inside in which the heated stones are placed

stone with charcoal and ash indicating the hearth is distinct from the debris from the hollow inside the sweat lodge which consists of larger heat-shattered stones only, without any charcoal or ash, such as those found near Langley Brook, downstream from a burnt mound.

The participation of contemporary sweat lodge users in the reconstructions drew attention to the ritual elements of the process which would not leave archaeological remains, and contributed to the interpretation of the archaeological evidence. Music, dancing and chanting take place while the stones are heating and before participants enter the sweat lodge. Used heated stones are regarded as special as is the site itself after abandonment. Sites are abandoned when they become muddy and unpleasant to use, and a new site might be established only a short distance away. This might explain the close proximity and indeed apparent clustering and pairing of burnt mounds.

Burnt mounds and Bronze Age settlements

There will no doubt continue to be debate over the function of burnt mounds but this must not distract attention from their wider significance in understanding the Bronze Age landscape of Birmingham. The information on people's impact on the environment provided by the types of deposits and plant and animal remains from Cob Lane has been described above. Whatever their function, burnt mounds may indicate the location, distribution and density of otherwise elusive contemporary settlements, which would be expected to be nearby but on slightly higher and drier ground than the burnt mound itself. Where the burnt mounds are on streams in parkland within the urban area, as at Cob Lane, Woodlands Park and Fox Hollies Park, this would be the land now occupied by modern houses on the edge of the park. As sweat lodges, burnt mounds need not have been within or adjacent to settlements, and their location would have been determined by the requirements of the process. Water would be required not only to produce steam, but a dammed stream could serve as a cold plunge after a sweat bath. The inaccessibility of some sites in particularly wet areas would have made them more mysterious and their location might in some cases have been deliberate.

Assuming that burnt mounds are related to settlements, and by comparison with 'Deverel-Rimbury' settlements in southern England which are contemporary with Birmingham's burnt mounds, Margaret Ehrenberg has suggested that settlements might be up to 50m away in any direction from the visible burnt mound; this is in addition to related features such as a sweat lodge which may be up to 10m away. The only settlement sites so far found in Birmingham that are potentially contemporary with a burnt mound are the enclosure at Langley Brook, 60m away from the burnt mound, and the earthworks noted close to the burnt mounds in Sutton Park. Excavation and geophysical survey has normally been restricted to the burnt mounds themselves and their immediate vicinity, so it is hardly surprising that no more contemporary settlements have been located, particularly if they are the sort of distance from burnt mounds suggested by Margaret Ehrenberg.

The tight cluster of all but one of the radiocarbon dates so far obtained for burnt mounds in Birmingham and its vicinity shows that many of the sites could have been in use at the same time. Together with the density of burnt mounds demonstrated by the surveys in south and north Birmingham and the landscape impact indicated at Cob Lane this suggests a substantial population, far more than had previously been thought.

The burnt mound phenomenon: between crisis and crisis?

Whether or not all or many of the burnt mounds were in use at the same time, and whatever their function, radiocarbon dates show that the burnt mound phenomenon in Birmingham may only have lasted for a few centuries. The process, technology or religion represented by burnt mounds seems to have arrived in the Birmingham area suddenly and disappeared suddenly. The evidence from Cob Lane and nearby sites shows that burnt mounds coincide with radical landscape change involving extensive clearance of forest and subsequent cultivation, probably related to population growth. Birmingham's burnt mounds appear at a time when land in other parts of the country was being parcelled up into extensive areas of fields or paddocks and presumably its use was being more closely controlled than hitherto: in southern England there are the so-called 'Celtic' fields, and on Dartmoor the 'reaves'. The relatively small quantity of Neolithic or earlier Bronze Age objects from Birmingham might mean that this was the first time that this area was intensively settled or farmed, as was the case on Dartmoor. The impetus for this process might have been pressure on resources created by an influx of people from another part of the country, who could have brought the burnt mound tradition with them.

The end of burnt mound use in Birmingham also coincides with changes in other parts of Britain, which include abandonment of settlements and fields, the construction of defended settlements and throwing weapons and other objects into wet areas. This may have been the result of several events, some or all of which were related: movement of people; soil exhaustion; a change to a wetter climate; and an environmental catastrophe in 1159 BC which has been detected in tree rings and is thought to have been caused by a massive eruption of the Hekla volcano. Reduced crop yields or even complete failure would have resulted in a reduction in population and wetter conditions might have made the burnt mounds, already in wet locations, difficult or impossible to use. The rise of a water religion indicated by the deposition of weapons might also have made wet areas sacred and prevented further use of burnt mounds. However, the burnt mounds might themselves have been part of water-related rituals.

In north Birmingham, the ditches of the streamside enclosure at Langley Brook were filled with alluvium resulting from the stream flooding the

22 Former stream channel at Peddimore, Sutton Coldfield

adjoining land. Flooding may also have occurred at Peddimore at this time, causing alluvial deposition. Cathy Mould's excavations revealed undated alluvium 30cm to 50cm (1ft to 1ft 8in) deep filling and sealing a former stream course *(22)*, which contains heat-shattered stones, possibly from a burnt mound, and nearby gullies. It is not yet known whether these are localised incidents or represent something more widespread.

IRON AGE BIRMINGHAM: A RURAL LANDSCAPE

In his *Iron Age Communities in Britain*, an overview of the period from about 700 BC to the Roman invasion of AD 43, Barry Cunliffe stated that the part of the country in which Birmingham lies

> ...is composed of vast tracts of Keuper marl [and] Triassic sandstones... highly unconducive to pre-Roman Iron Age settlement. Apart from the river gravels and the more fertile sandstone and limestone hills, much of the area appears, on present evidence, to have been largely unsettled.

This statement was originally written in 1974 but repeated as recently as 1991. It reflects, as in other periods of Birmingham's past, a false perception of how the geological formations influenced past land use, a lack of prominent surviving features, a lack until recently of much archaeological work, and an assumption that the type of archaeological sites and the density of sites are necessarily comparable with those in other parts of Britain where more archaeological work has taken place.

No hillforts, the defended hill-top enclosures characteristic of this period in western and southern Britain and often still prominent features of the landscape, have yet been found in Birmingham itself. There are three hillforts just outside the city: Castle Old Fort in Brownhills to the north-west, Wychbury Hill in Hagley to the south-west and Berry Mound to the south. The locations of others near Birmingham are suggested by earthworks at Dudley Castle and place names, topography and antiquarian accounts at Wednesbury, Oldbury and Barr Beacon. Loaches Banks, just outside the city boundary to the north-west, may be Iron Age in date. It consists of three banks and ditches surrounding a roughly rectangular area on a low rise near a stream. At Wishaw Hall Farm excavations on the line of the M6 Toll motorway revealed an Iron Age boundary consisting of a line of square pits, which was later replaced by a segmented ditch. The alignment was maintained into the Roman period. There was also a curving gully further south which may have been Iron Age.

Until 2001, the only evidence for Birmingham's Iron Age was a glass bead dating to the second century BC from Bromford, a few sherds of probable Iron Age pottery from Selly Park and Kings Norton and a sherd from the Roman fort at Metchley. In that year, excavations at Langley Mill Farm in Sutton Coldfield on the line of the M6 Toll motorway revealed an Iron Age farm *(23)*.

The site was originally indicated by a small quantity of debris from flint tool making in the Mesolithic period, but a geophysical survey revealed the lines of ditches and subsequent trenching showed that some of the ditches contained heat-shattered stones and Roman pottery. Large-scale excavation by Oxford Wessex Archaeology revealed the Iron Age farm, adjoining the five ditched enclosures of Roman date described in the next chapter.

The Iron Age farm, on a slope running down to Langley Brook, consisted of circular timber houses in a roughly square area about 65m across, bounded by a V-shaped ditch over a metre deep with a gap on its north side providing an entrance *(24)*. It contained seven curving gullies which would have surrounded circular timber houses up to 10m in diameter and acted as ground-level gutters, taking rainwater dripping from the eaves of their roofs *(25)*. One of the gullies was overlapped by two others, indicating that what may have been the main dwelling house was rebuilt twice. Several other post holes outside the houses show that there were other timber structures in the farmyard. This site is dated by a small quantity (20 sherds) of Iron Age pottery and by radiocarbon to sometime between the third and first centuries BC. An amber bead was the only decorative item. A circular stone which

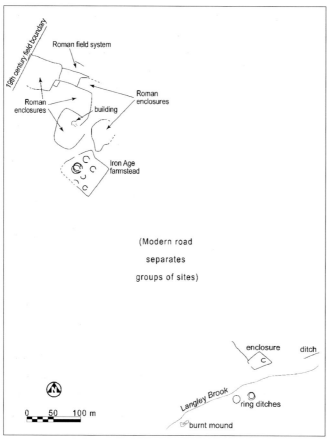

19th century field boundary

Roman field system

Roman enclosures

building

Roman enclosures

Iron Age farmstead

(Modern road

separates

groups of sites)

enclosure   ditch

C

Langley Brook   ring ditches

burnt mound

0   50   100 m

23 Left Prehistoric and Roman sites near Langley Mill Farm. *Redrawn from drawings by Oxford Wessex Archaeology, with permission of Midlands Expressway Limited*

24 Below Ditch of the Iron Age farm at Langley Mill Farm

25 Opposite Gully surrounding a circular house in the Iron Age Farm at Langley Mill Farm. Segments of the infilled gully have been excavated

was found in the ditch surrounding the farmstead is the base of a hand quern used to grind grain *(26)*, but cereals were not necessarily grown here. As in the Roman enclosures which succeeded it, livestock – probably cattle – may have been the mainstay of this farm, but unfortunately animal bone does not survive in the acid soil on this site. The ditch around the farm would have been accompanied by an earth bank and fence. It would have kept livestock in or out and would have deterred wild animals and unwanted human visitors, but may have been primarily a symbol of the status, or assumed status, of the farm's occupants – an Iron Age version of the numerous moated farmsteads of medieval Birmingham, described in Chapter 4.

The Langley Mill site is similar to Iron Age farms along the River Tame north of Birmingham. It may have been, like them, part of a landscape which consisted of enclosures at intervals with ditched fields around, although no ditched fields in neighbouring Warwickshire have yet been dated before the Roman period. The smaller enclosure near Langley Brook to its south-east, containing a gully surrounding a circular house, is also Iron Age in date and therefore part of this landscape *(10)*. The Bromford glass bead and the Iron Age pottery from Kings Norton and Selly Park may indicate other farmsteads like this in Birmingham. This would be the landscape encountered by the Roman army about AD 47. Another piece of Birmingham's Iron Age landscape, 2.5km (1.5 miles) long and 5m (about 16ft 9in) wide, is buried under the road built by that army in Sutton Park. Excavations across the road in 1936 revealed that it lay on a soil known as a *podzol*, in which the nutrients have been washed down through the soil leaving it acidic and a pale grey colour. This is just the

26 Base of a quern from the ditch of the Iron Age farm at Langley Mill Farm

type of soil in most of Sutton Park today, and shows that the types of heath and woodland vegetation that grow on it now would have been there in the first century AD as well. As in its more recent past, trees, heather, gorse and bracken would have been exploited for various purposes and the land would have been used for grazing animals rather than growing crops.

We do not know what the inhabitants of Iron Age Birmingham called themselves or what their tribal affiliations were. Of the tribal groups recognised by the Roman administration, the Corieltauvi were to the east, the Cornovii to the north-west and the Dobunni to the south-west and Birmingham may be at the junction of the territories of all three. This may explain the location of the Roman fort at Metchley.

CHAPTER 3
BIRMINGHAM IN THE ROMAN EMPIRE AND BEYOND

In AD 43 an army of conquest under the command of Aulus Plautius landed on the south coast. Just a few years later, a Roman fort was built on a site that is now partly occupied by the campus and Medical School of the University of Birmingham and partly by the Queen Elizabeth Hospital at Metchley in Edgbaston. This brought what is now Birmingham into the Roman Empire.

Although there was never a Roman town of Birmingham, several sites of this period are now known within the city, providing evidence for soldiers, farmers and Birmingham's first industries (27). The earliest excavations at the fort at Metchley took place in the 1930s but much new information has been obtained from recent extensive excavations here, which also discovered Birmingham's first village just outside the fort. A farmstead or small rural settlement in Kings Norton and one of the sites excavated on the line of the M6 Toll motorway have provided a glimpse into the Roman countryside, and other farms have been identified from concentrations of pottery on field surfaces in Sutton Coldfield. Two pottery kilns have been found, and the lines of at least three Roman roads pass through the city. Buried ground surfaces, pollen, charred seeds and beetles, in addition to manmade structures and objects, provide evidence of the surrounding environment and of the exploitation and management of resources.

We cannot treat the Birmingham sites in isolation but must relate them to the history of Roman Britain as a whole and its political and economic systems. Imperial administration and physical structures were imposed on people living in the area but at the same time these people had access to a market economy whose demands must have stimulated agricultural and industrial activity, possibly leading to specialised production. By bringing together the evidence for Roman Birmingham in a chronological sequence and considering its relationship to what went before we can begin to assess the impact of the area's incorporation into the Empire. We can also throw at least a little light on Birmingham's Dark Ages that followed.

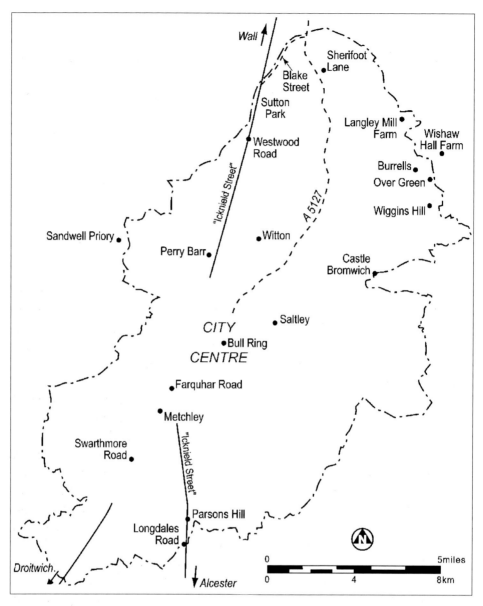

Wall

Sherifoot
Lane

Blake
Street

Sutton
Park

Langley Mill
Farm

Wishaw
Hall Farm

Westwood
Road

"Icknield Street"

A5127

Burrells

Over Green

Wiggins Hill

Sandwell Priory

Witton

Perry Barr

Castle
Bromwich

CITY

Saltley

Bull Ring

CENTRE

Farquhar Road

Metchley

Swarthmore
Road

"Icknield Street"

Parsons Hill

Longdales
Road

Droitwich

Alcester

N

0   5miles
0   4   8km

27 Roman sites mentioned in the text (find spots of individual objects are not shown). *Based
on the Ordnance Survey map and reproduced by permission of Ordnance Survey on behalf of
the Controller of Her Majesty's Stationery Office, © Crown Copyright 100042011*

THE CONQUEST: FORTS

The Roman fort at Metchley in Edgbaston was established about AD 48 and occupied until about AD 200, having undergone various phases of modification of its defences and internal structures, including periods of abandonment. In its earliest phases there was a *vicus* or civilian settlement outside the fort. We do not know the Roman name of the fort, and probably never will. The history of the fort at Metchley as revealed by excavation relates to other forts in the region and to the military history of Roman Britain as a whole.

With the exception of a short length of ditch, all of the archaeological remains of the Roman fort at Metchley are now below ground. Although its defences remained visible into the twentieth century and clearly formed the characteristic 'playing card' shape, Birmingham's Roman fort was not fully accepted as such until demonstrated by excavations in 1934. The historian William Hutton thought that it was too large for a Roman fort and must be the work of the Danes, and nineteenth and early twentieth century Ordnance Survey maps label the site as 'Supposed Roman camp' *(28)*. The excavations of Keith St Joseph and Fred Shotton in 1934 were prompted by the discovery of Roman pottery during the construction of the University of Birmingham's Medical School on one corner of the fort. St Joseph and Shotton dug trenches across the defences and also located an entrance to the fort on its west side, with a pebble roadway leading through it. They identified two phases of development and suggested, from the pottery they found, that the fort had been occupied for a short period only. Further work took place in the 1940s and in 1950 Graham Webster excavated the north-west corner, finding a timber corner tower. A trench was dug across the western defences in 1963. In 1967-69 Trevor Rowley's excavations examined the defences and parts of the interior of the fort near its north-west and south-western corners. These showed that there were three or four phases of construction and use of the fort, but that all of these were within the first century AD.

More recently, excavations by Alex Jones and Birmingham Archaeology since 1997 as part of new development have demonstrated that the fort was larger, had more phases of construction and was occupied for a longer period than previously thought. These have included large areas in the south and east of the fort within the university campus, exploratory trenches and test pits in the northern part of the fort, and an area outside the west of the fort which located and investigated a *vicus* or civilian settlement. Alex Jones has also analysed and published the results of the 1960s excavations. About 25 per cent of the fort has been excavated.

The fort occupies a plateau which is overlooked by higher ground to the north-west but slopes steeply on the other three sides down to streams that would have provided a water supply for the garrison. Marshy ground around the streams would also have formed an additional defence. The first fort on the

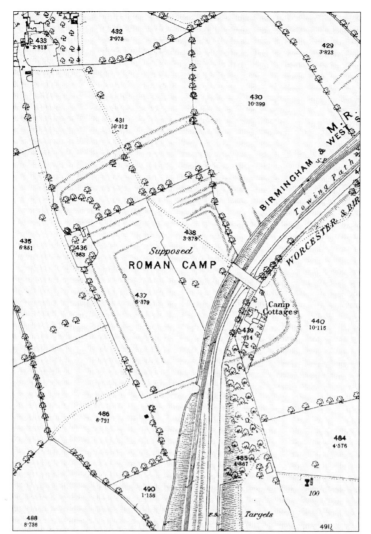

28 Metchley Roman fort as shown on the 1890 Ordnance Survey map, with its banks and ditches clearly marked

site (*29*, Phase 1) was established in the late 40s AD and is contemporary with forts at Droitwich, Alcester, Greensforge near Kinver, Penkridge, Mancetter and possibly Wall. It was about 200m square and was defended by double ditches *(30)* and a turf rampart with a timber fence or palisade on top of it. There was a gully in the base of the ditch which may also have held a palisade. A gravel roadway ran out of the fort's west gate, and military ditches outside the western defences of the first fort and under the vicus may be part of a *titulum* or short line of rampart and ditch in front of the gateway. Alternatively they might be temporary defences used while the fort was being constructed.

The fort's garrison would have been about 1,000 men and probably included cavalry. Excavations revealed remains of timber buildings inside the fort at this period which can be interpreted as barrack blocks, two granaries,

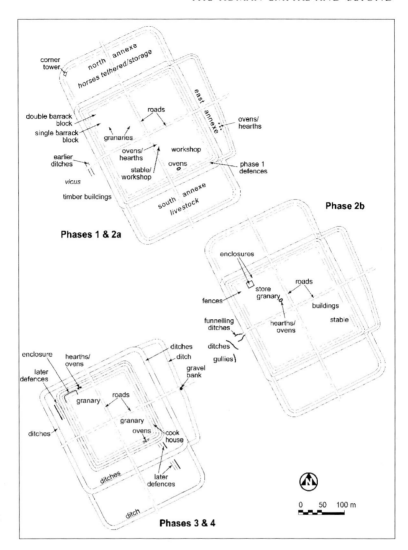

29 Schematic plans of different phases at Metchley Roman forts

workshops and a store building. All of the buildings were based on horizontal beams resting in trenches in the ground. One of the barrack blocks was of a standard and distinctive form, a long rectangular building most of which was divided into ten paired rooms, each pair forming the sleeping quarters and storage area respectively for a group of eight men, with private quarters for the centurion at one end. It had a verandah along one side. The other barrack block was an unusual doubled version of this (a back-to-back arrangement nearly 1,800 years before Birmingham's other back-to-back houses, described in chapter 5), with rooms in rows of four. The granaries rested on large horizontal timber beams which raised them off the ground to deter vermin and keep the grain dry. In the south-east part of the fort there was a building which might have been a smith's workshop because it contained circular flat-based

30 Excavations across the double ditches of the first phase fort at Metchley. Recuts are visible
in the far (inner) ditch

pits, possibly part of furnaces used in metalworking. Another building near
the centre of the fort and next to the main north–south road was divided into
stalls suggesting it may have been a stable. Hearths and ovens were sensibly
placed outside timber buildings, just inside the rampart, and were identified by
the burnt clay and charcoal filling them. Two of three bowl-shaped ovens or
hearths just inside the southern defences of the fort were probably bread ovens
since charred barley and wheat grains were found in the fort's outer ditch; the
third contained smithing debris suggesting iron working.

Soon after it was established there were changes in the layout of the fort's
buildings and annexes were constructed on the fort's north, east and south
sides (*29*, Phase 2a). The enlargement of the Metchley fort, about AD 50, is
contemporary with the rebuilding of existing forts in the region and establishment of some new ones.

One of the barrack blocks was divided by corridors into three partly
self-contained units, which would have increased storage space but reduced
accommodation for the garrison. The northern annexe was defended by a
double ditch and a rampart with a timber fence on it, including a tower at
the north-western corner, the eastern by a single ditch and rampart (*31*), and
the southern by a double ditch. Charcoal and burnt daub in the trenches cut
to remove the posts of the north-west corner tower when it was dismantled
showed that the tower and fences were faced with clay-covered woven

31 Excavated segments through the ditch around the eastern annexe at Metchley Roman fort. The outer ditch of the main fort runs under the hedge and buildings on the right

wattles. No remains of any structures were found during excavation of the northern annexe, suggesting that it may have been used for storage or that horses were tethered here. A break in the rampart of the eastern annexe and post holes may represent an entrance and two ditches beyond its line may have been outer defences, possibly containing hedges. Within the eastern annexe, there were a pebbled yard and flat-based ovens or hearths which were possibly used for baking bread. One of them contained peas and beans as well as wheat and barley, the vegetable part of the soldiers' diet. The ditch of the eastern annexe also contained charred wheat and barley grain.

Two shallow drainage gullies at the back of the annexe's rampart were overlain by hearths or ovens filled with charcoal which suggest industrial activity. Siting these away from the timber buildings inside the main fort would have reduced the fire risk. Most of the southern annexe is occupied by modern buildings which would have removed any remains of internal features. However, dung beetles in the adjoining outer ditch of the main fort suggest that animals were kept in the annexe.

A civilian settlement or *vicus* was established just outside the fort's west gate. It consisted of open-fronted timber-framed buildings, probably shops, which were alongside and spread onto the gravel trackway leading out of the gate. In addition there was an outlying building, probably a dwelling, with two phases of flooring. The occupants of the *vicus* would have included people following the garrison on campaign, soldiers' families, and local people who were attracted by the trading opportunities that the military garrison offered. It would have given soldiers the opportunity to buy foodstuffs not provided in the military ration and provided services like a tavern and brothel. The excavated *vicus* may not have been the only or even principal *vicus* at Metchley. There may have been others outside other gates of the fort, particularly the south, but any remains of them in each of these areas will have been severely affected by twentieth-century buildings.

At a later stage the buildings in the *vicus* were replaced by ditches forming a funnel shape converging on the fort's western entrance, possibly for herding livestock into the fort. The ditches were subsequently cut across by curving ditches forming an annexe or outer enclosure here. Gullies to the west may indicate further buildings.

Probably at the same time as the *vicus* was abandoned, the buildings inside the fort were demolished and burnt, and replaced by small timber-framed buildings, hearths and ovens for metalworking and ditched and fenced enclosures (*29*, Phase 2b). The buildings in the north-west of the fort included a possible granary and store building. There was a small rectangular building just inside the eastern side of the fort, and a possible stable in the south-east corner. Near the centre there was part of a clay-floored building, and a timber-framed building with an irregular layout. Lines of stakeholes probably indicate wattle fences. The buildings and enclosures inside the fort and the funnelling ditches outside are more like what we would expect to see in an agricultural settlement than in a military establishment and suggest that the fort may have become a storage depot for crops and livestock. It could have served other forts in the area that remained garrisoned. The irregular layout of the buildings compared to those of earlier phases suggests that poorer quality timber was used: rather than long straight lengths, the irregular plans indicate curving timbers. This may have been because the buildings did not merit the use of good quality timber, or because there were no longer suitable trees in the vicinity.

Later, and probably in the 60s AD, the site was refortified when a smaller fort was built inside the earlier defences (*29*, Phase 3). As for the earlier periods of Metchley's history, defences and buildings were refurbished or newly constructed at this period at other forts in the region such as Wall, Mancetter and Baginton. This renewed activity may have been part of a campaign of pacification and regaining control following the revolt of Boudicca.

The new defences at Metchley consisted of a rampart and ditch inside the earlier forts, but both the earlier forts' double ditches and the east side of the southern annexe were cleaned out to serve as an outer defence. The eastern annexe ditch was also cleaned out and a dump of gravel formed a causeway across it. The rampart of the new fort was built of turves which contained pollen of alder, birch, hazel, grass and fern, with some heather. This suggests that there were patches of woodland, possibly managed as coppice, amongst areas of open land, including heathland.

On the north and west sides of the fort the turf rampart was fronted with vertical timbers. There were probably timber towers at regular intervals along it. On the east and south sides a triangular arrangement of timbers formed a bracing. The west side of the fort's north gate, in a gap in the rampart and ditch, consisted of six large posts, each about 23cm (9in) square. The north-south road of the earlier forts was resurfaced where it ran through the new north gate, and a road surface was traced extending for 12m outside the west gate. A road running along the inside of the rampart on the northern side would have continued along the entire circuit. The only buildings found in the interior were a granary in the north-west and another in the south-east, and a possible cookhouse with adjoining hearth in the south-east. Near this, just inside the defences on the south side, there were pits containing charcoal and burnt clay together with charred grains of wheat and barley indicating that they were probably ovens used for baking bread. Other ovens were found just inside the rampart on the northern side of the fort.

Later still, more defences were constructed, including a ditch on the western side of the fort on a different alignment to the earlier defences and a rampart and double ditches to the south-east (29, phase 4). Pottery from the eastern annexe shows that the site was occupied into the second century, and hooked rims from Severn Valley ware jars may even date to the third century. However, there is very little black-burnished ware, which occurs in large quantities on military sites occupied in the early second century, showing that the military occupation of Metchley had ceased by then. The function of the site after the first century is discussed below.

As large parts of the defences were still visible as earthworks into the early part of the twentieth century it is not surprising that fairly recent pottery occurs in the upper parts of the ditches, but the outer ditch of the phase one fort and the eastern annexe ditch were deliberately cleaned out as part of the boundary of a hunting lodge in the eighteenth-century Metchley Park.

The pottery from the fort not only dates the various phases but also indicates that the site was supplied from local and distant sources. Some pottery was being made on or near the site itself. Most of the pottery from the site is dateable to AD 45-70 but there is also pottery dating to the late first to early second century and even to the later second or third century.

The first-century pottery announces the arrival of a foreign army from an empire occupying the west and south of continental Europe. It includes *mortaria* or mixing bowls from north Gaul, glossy red samian tableware from south and central Gaul, beakers and cups from Lyon, flagons found on sites in the Rhineland and large double-handled amphorae which would have contained olive oil from southern Spain.

The occurrence of 'tubby' cooking pots from the Malverns, handmade vessels whose form dates back to the pre-Roman Iron Age, shows that the Roman army was also acquiring pottery from local producers. Storage jars, also probably from the Malvern area, may have been containers for salt. There were also tankards and jars of the orange-coloured Severn Valley ware and grey wares. *Mortaria* or mixing bowls used at Metchley came from Verulamium near St Albans, Mancetter in north Warwickshire and Littlechester near Derby. One piece of *mortarium* is stamped with the name of its maker, Septuminus, who worked at both Mancetter and Littlechester and can be dated to the end of the first century or beginning of the second. However, the majority of the *mortaria*, and possibly the flagons, were probably made on or close to the fort itself and the discovery of fragments of misfired pottery and a potter's kick wheel of lava from the Rhineland also indicates potting on the site.

In addition to pottery, fragments of glass bowls, beakers and bottles were found. Metal objects include copper alloy brooches and a small bronze dog, which probably decorated a handle. There was also the head of an iron entrenching tool, which might have been used to dig out the fort's ditches. Quern-stones of Pennine millstone grit were part of hand mills used to grind the cereals whose presence on the site is indicated by charred grain. Glass gaming counters illustrate how bored and probably homesick soldiers occupied their time. We do not know where they came from, but it would have been from within and probably near the frontiers of the Empire.

In the later first century AD most forts in the West Midlands were abandoned when the army was campaigning in Wales and northern Britain but there was some military activity in the second century at Wall, Droitwich and Alcester. What was the function of Metchley in its later phases, which are indicated by defences and pottery showing occupation up to the end of the second century? The tree pollen in turf used for the rampart of the third fort might indicate gradual encroachment of woodland around the fort and similarly pollen from the outer fort ditch indicates a transition from an open landscape to increasing woodland in the later Roman period.

Retained in government ownership, the site could have become a *mansio* or inn, but we may be wrong in regarding the ditches of this phase as defensive. They may have formed a stock enclosure or enclosures for a neighbouring but as yet unlocated farm. As suggested below, Metchley's role as a local administrative centre may have been taken over by the site at Longdales Road.

Metchley is as yet the only Roman fort known in Birmingham. The antiquary Christopher Chattock, writing in 1884, suggested that there was a Roman fort at Holford where the road from Metchley to Wall, described below, crossed the River Tame but there is little evidence to support this other than the site's topography, a plateau overlooking the river. Roman coins, mainly of Constantine, have been found on the site, possibly indicating a civilian Roman settlement at a later date.

THE CONQUEST: ROADS

Metchley fort was part of a network of forts established across the West Midlands in the middle of the first century AD. It was linked by roads to Wall to the north, Alcester to the south and Droitwich to the south-west. There may also have been roads to Greensforge to the west, Penkridge to the north-west and Mancetter to the north-east. The roads to Alcester and Wall and beyond to the north-east and south-west were given the name Icknield Street in the medieval period, misleadingly implying that it was a single road rather than individual stretches linking forts. However, as this name and its variants such as Ryknild and Rycknield have been in use for some time, I am using it here for these particular stretches of road. As with Metchley fort, we do not know the Roman names of any of these roads.

The exact lines of these roads in the immediate vicinity of Metchley are not known and it is difficult to trace the original lines of roads where they are in present built-up areas. Peter Leather and the Birmingham Roman Roads Research Project have boldly attempted to locate road lines where they pass through small open spaces within the conurbation, mainly by resistance survey, unfortunately with little success. However, a visual and resistivity survey at Lickey Hills on the south side of Birmingham may have identified the final sighting point on the route from Droitwich to Metchley and therefore established its line within the city. Even before recent urban development Roman roads would be susceptible to removal by cultivation once they went out of use. Near Wall, for example, recent excavations revealed only the side ditches of Icknield Street. The *agger* or cambered gravel road surface had only survived in a field boundary. In Westwood Road, just south of Sutton Park where the Icknield Street survives in an extremely good state of preservation, as described below, no trace of the road was found in an excavation in what is now a house garden. Along Chester Road North, just outside Sutton Park, the road survives as no more than patches of gravel and dry areas in gardens. The discovery of a roadside ditch confirmed that part of Wellhead Lane in Perry Barr is on the line of Icknield Street.

In 1955 Adrian Oswald observed what he interpreted as a gravel road 60cm (2ft) thick on the line of Icknield Street in Farquhar Road north of Metchley, but a gravelly deposit about 0.28m (11in) thick exposed during construction work on an adjoining site in 1995 may have been a natural formation, casting some doubt on whether the feature observed by Oswald was actually a road. A similar gravel spread was observed in a water pipe trench nearby in 2002, together with a feature that could have been a roadside ditch. To the south of Metchley, the features observed by Robert Hetherington in Swarthmore Road in 1963 during development are far more convincing but unfortunately the road was not aligned on Metchley and may have served some other purpose. He recorded a metalled *agger* flanked by wide quarry ditches and identified six periods of construction, five of them Roman, including one or more periods

32 The *agger* of the Roman road in Sutton Park

when the gravel road was laid over the former quarry ditch. The *agger* overlay a rutted natural clay surface, which was overlaid by layers of trampled clay and gravel, then a layer of sandy loam with a thin band of wood ash over it.

A well-preserved stretch of the Roman road that joined the fort at Metchley to that at Wall near Lichfield, and is usually known as Icknield Street, survives in Sutton Park *(32)*. The historian William Hutton, on seeing it for the first time in November 1762, wrote

> I thought it the grandest site I had ever beheld; and was amazed, so noble a monument should be so little regarded.

It is unfortunately still little regarded in national terms and does not feature in nationally-based guides to archaeological sites but its excellent state of preservation provides much information on Roman road construction and on the first-century landscape through which it was constructed. It is a good example of a gravel and pebble Roman road, in contrast to the more famous 'paved' Roman roads such as Wheeldale Moor in North Yorkshire whose 'paving' would originally have been covered with gravel, and Blackstone Edge in West Yorkshire which is now thought to be of a later date.

The 1½-mile length of the road in the Park owes its survival to its incorporation into a deer park created by 1126, described below. The deer park's ditch and bank boundary runs just to the west of the road. The road had become a parish boundary, presumably in the Anglo-Saxon period, because it was the only clear feature in a heathland landscape, and it remained the county boundary between Warwickshire and Staffordshire into the nineteenth century.

As Hutton and other observers have noted, the road is 18m (60ft) wide between two side ditches, and consists of three parts, the *agger* up to 9m (30ft) wide and 0.3m to 1m high (1 to 3ft), and a strip 4m (13ft) wide on each side of it separating it from side ditches. In national terms the width of the road places it in the second class of roads defined by Ivan Margary. Beyond the side ditches on each side of the road, as Hutton observed, there are a number of pits, from which gravel was dug to construct the road *(33)*. Hutton went on to infer that the area was well-wooded when the road was built and that the pits were dug between trees which were left in place.

Excavations have shown that the road was not composed of a series of graded layers, which many textbooks describe as the normal method of construction of Roman roads, but that its form was determined by the availability of local resources, which varied even within Sutton Park. It consists of a dump of unsorted compacted gravel or gravel and pebbles, with a gravel capping but never any sort of paved surface. In places it had a foundation layer of larger stones.

33 A quarry pit alongside the Roman road in Sutton Park

The earliest recorded excavation on the road took place before 1860, when it is described by Agnes Bracken in her *History of the Forest and Chase of Sutton Coldfield*. It exposed the 'broken stones, which formed its solid foundation'. Excavations by 'Glowworm' in 1885 or earlier, possibly those mentioned by Bracken, revealed 20cm (8in) of topsoil below the turf, overlying about 20cm (8in) of well-laid pebbles or gravel. In 1936 Benjamin Walker dug a trench across the road in the south part of the park and dug a pit into it in the north part. In the south, he showed that the raised part of the road, the *agger*, was 9m (30 ft) wide with a steep camber and was composed of compacted gravel and pebbles about 30cm (1ft) thick with a surface of finer gravel. The line of his trench is still visible as a spade's width hollow running at an angle to the road line. In the northern part of the park, where the road is lower, there was a capping of pebbles 7.5cm (3in) thick over 23cm (9in) of earth and pebbles. This in turn overlay the ground surface that existed when the road was constructed: black, peaty sand 15cm (6in) thick over grey sand and pebbles. Pits dug in a similar location in 1982 to sample the buried ground surface showed that the road surface was 40cm (16in). The black peaty layer under it was 10cm (4in) thick over grey sand which was itself 10cm (4in) thick and overlay a yellow sand. In 1979 David Symons observed a sewer pipe trench dug through the road and recorded large water-worn stones, which he interpreted as the base of the road.

I carried out a detailed survey in 1977 after a major fire had cleared much of the vegetation on and around the road. This included drawn profiles of the road which showed that the height of the *agger* decreased from about 60cm (2ft) in the south to about 40cm (16in) in the north *(34)*. Here, as Walker's 1936 trench showed, fewer pebbles were used, because they were buried by peat and therefore more difficult to obtain. There is a marked absence of quarry pits on the eastern side of the road here although they occur on both sides elsewhere in the park. Where the road runs through woodland this has deterred use of the *agger* as a footpath and subsequent erosion, and it has retained a markedly convex profile. The side ditches are each about 2m wide and intermittent rather than continuous. They were not for drainage but were laying-out lines dug by Roman surveyors to mark where vegetation would have to be cleared to construct the road. As Hutton suggested, the gaps between lengths of ditches probably show where vegetation was left uncleared, but as discussed above, the soil under the road shows that the area was woodland or heathland, so perhaps the gaps were gorse bushes or dense stands of heather or bracken rather than trees.

The Metchley fort and the network of known Roman roads were constructed for military purposes, not for the benefit or convenience of the existing population, and were imposed on an existing landscape that was far from empty. Some of the Roman road lines in the area are followed by modern roads and others are visible as disused lines, most notably in Sutton

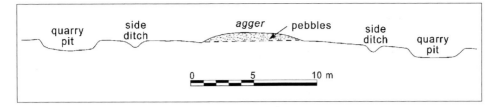

34 Cross-section of the Roman road in Sutton Park, combining Benjamin Walker's excavated section of 1936 with profiles measured in 1977

Park. Possible changes in alignment during the Roman period have been suggested, but at least those stretches of road still in use must have been used after their function as military communication lines had passed. There would have been many other trackways, often on more logical natural routes. The local population would have been using these routes at the time of the Roman conquest and may have preferred them to the better but less convenient roads, which might nonetheless have seen official traffic.

Assuming they were dropped by travellers, coins of Constantine found along the road in Sutton Park suggest that it was still in use in the fourth century, but the natural route along the sandstone ridge running north from Birmingham to Sutton Coldfield and Lichfield, most of which is now the A5127, was probably in use before the Roman road was built and remained a preferred route during the Roman period. The location of the pottery kiln at Sherifoot Lane, discussed below, can be explained by the existence of a road on this line. To the north of Sutton Park, just south of its junction with Watling Street and near Wall, excavations revealed that the parallel side ditches of Icknield Street formed part of enclosures around burial areas. Inhumation burials show that the cemetery was used into the third century AD, but this does not prove that the whole road remained in use at this date because this stretch may have provided access from Wall, along Watling Street, to the cemetery only. Immediately north of Sutton Park, the line of the Icknield Street crosses very wet ground around Footherley. This could have been avoided by cutting along Blake Street, which is known to have existed in the medieval period, to the ridgeway route followed by the A5127.

FARMS AND FIELDS

The *vicus* or civilian settlement outside the Metchley fort is not typical of other Roman settlements in the area. It was physically and economically linked to the fort, and was a nucleated village, a settlement type foreign to this area at that time. Most people would have been living in farmsteads like the Iron Age site at Langley Mill Farm described above.

The evidence for the rural landscape of Birmingham in the Roman period consists of the excavated remains of settlements with the boundaries of their fields and paddocks, Roman pottery on field surfaces, some visible field boundaries and charred seeds of wheat, barley, peas and beans from Metchley fort which were probably grown in its vicinity. The existing evidence indicates a potentially large number of settlements, as little as 1km (0.6 mile) apart. In the north of the area these may have used relatively little pottery, which makes them difficult to locate. The proximity of Roman settlements to known medieval settlements suggests that the latter may be on the same site as their Roman predecessors.

Although we describe these settlements as 'Roman', the people who lived on them were not necessarily immigrants. In many if not most cases they were probably descendants of the families who were there before the Roman conquest.

At the second-century pottery kiln site in Perry Barr, described below, late first- and early second-century pottery indicates earlier occupation but no structures of this period were found. The site at Parsons Hill in Kings Norton was discovered in 1949 when Michael Nixon noticed Roman pottery in the side of a trackway. Subsequent excavation revealed sloping gravel surfaces and narrow gullies. The gravel surfaces were covered with layers containing charcoal, daub, and pottery of first to third century date. The charcoal and daub indicate timber buildings, and the gullies could have been slots for wall beams or drainage ditches. The pebble surfaces could be part of a road surface: the likely line of the Icknield Street would go through this site. A ditch containing first and second pottery, probably a field boundary, was found nearby in 2006.

Only 1km south of Parsons Hill, and also close to the line of the Icknield Street, in this case a stretch still in use, Josh Williams's recent excavations at Longdales Road in Kings Norton, in 2002 and 2003, revealed part of a Roman rural landscape consisting of features extending over an area at least 300m long and 300m wide in a raised location (35). A large triple-ditched enclosure measuring about 70m by 60m contained pebble surfaces, a circular and a rectangular timber building but no other recognisable structures. The enclosure succeeded an earlier phase of occupation on the site which consisted of ditches, some of which were straight and are likely to have been field boundaries and others which were curving and may have been gullies around houses. There were also possible fence lines and pits, including one which contained heat-shattered stones but no charcoal. The enclosure ditches were up to 2m wide and up to 0.7m (28in) deep (36). The outer two were V-shaped and wider and deeper than the inner. There may originally have been banks between the ditches. There was possibly a smaller enclosure on the western side of the inner enclosure. An extensive pebble surface in the eastern part of the inner enclosure had a patch of burning on its surface, and beam slots adjoining it suggest a rectangular timber building. The only other structure was a ring

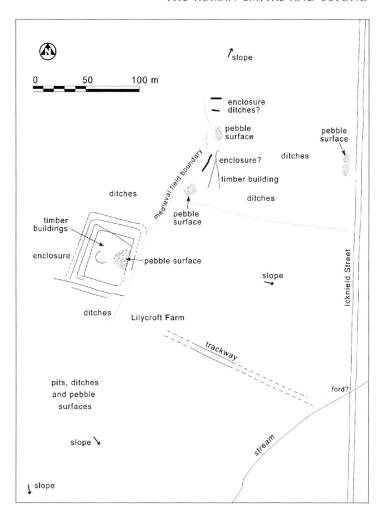

35 Longdales Road Roman sites. *Redrawn from plans by Birmingham Archaeology and Worcestershire County Council Historic Environment and Archaeology Service*

gully about 10m in diameter. Parts of the pebble surface, particularly towards its edges, could be the floors of buildings whose walls were based on ground beams that have left no traces. In a subsequent phase, a pit was cut through the fill of the inner enclosure ditch and a series of gullies were dug.

Further gullies and ditches beyond the enclosure may be the boundaries of fields and paddocks around it. Just outside the present city boundary, Chris Patrick's trenching revealed a pebble trackway 8m wide with a ditch on each side leading up to the enclosure from the south east, possibly from a stream about 200m away, and probably entered the enclosure on its southeast side. To its south, a single trench located gullies, pits, a pebble surface and post holes representing a timber building. To the north of the enclosure, excavations revealed further ditches, pebble surfaces *(37)* and remains of timber buildings. Some of the ditches, particularly a pair of ditches at the extreme north end of the excavated area which are like the outer two ditches of the large

36 The large Roman enclosure at Longdales Road. The outer ditch is visible in the foreground. The other side of the enclosure is on the far side of the excavated area

37 A pebble surface at Longdales Road, north of the large enclosure

enclosure described above, may themselves have bounded another enclosure, and converging ditches in the south may have been used to control livestock. There were charred spelt wheat grains on one of the pebble surfaces, some of which had sprouted, suggesting malting for ale production. The building remains included trenches for the wall beams of a small timber building, another ring gully and a large rectangular structure 4m wide, whose posts rested on pebble bases and which may have been a barn. Pebble surfaces and ditches were also found alongside Icknield Street to the east of the enclosure. Tracks and ditches bounded large rectangular paddocks at right angles to Icknield Street, containing circular houses. Existing hedges follow the Roman land divisions.

Many pieces of pottery had been thrown into the ditches of the enclosure and trampled into the pebble surfaces inside and to the north of it. The bulk of the pottery is second to fourth century in date, and is the sort of pottery which would have been in everyday use on settlements of this date. Most of it had been made in the West Midlands, and included bowls and tankards in orange Severn Valley ware, the type which was made in the kiln at Perry Barr and many places to the south and west of Birmingham, and *mortaria* or mixing bowls made in north Warwickshire. There were just a few pieces of pots made further field like glossy red Samian tableware from Gaul and amphorae from the Mediterranean. The acid soil was unfortunately not conducive to bone survival.

How can we explain this site? The enclosure is in a prominent location next to the Icknield Street and next to a farm which is known from documentary evidence to have been there in AD 1314. It has a clear view to the site of the fort at Metchley. The size of the enclosure is greater than we would expect for a single farmstead. The ditches of the enclosure and other ditches on the site would have kept in livestock, but three ditches seem excessive. Stock would have required water: there is a stream not far from the main enclosure, but the site is on a clayey soil in which rainwater ponds up. Large pits could have been dug as waterholes, and some of the ditches might have been for drainage. The cobble surfaces would have provided a firm surface for people and animals. The ditches of the enclosure and other ditches to its north, which may surround another enclosure, were cut to a V-shape, something we might associate with a fort rather than a farm, but there was nothing else on the site which suggests it is military. Perhaps there was a fear of theft of livestock or other possessions at a time when neighbouring Gaul was suffering from wandering brigands or *Bacaudae*. The site could have served as a collecting and storage depot for animals and crops from surrounding farms, before they or their products were sent along the road to the Roman town at Alcester. Livestock would have been kept in the ditched enclosure. Cattle or sheep might have gone on the hoof to market, sheep may have been shorn here and their fleeces taken or animals could have been milked and dairy products made. The barn might have been for grain similarly collected from several farms, or could have stored fodder for the livestock.

There is a much greater quantity of pottery from this site, and from the Parsons Hill site considering the small area excavated, than from Roman sites in the north of Birmingham. Did the proximity to a road make pottery, particularly Severn Valley ware, more easily obtainable or did it mean that the settlement was generally more Romanised because of the influence of traffic, including official traffic, to and from places like Alcester? The quantity of pottery might simply show the intensity of activity, but other than ditches the main features appear to be pebbled yards rather than buildings. As well as a collecting point, the site might have served as a rural roadside market, serving scattered farms whose nearest market would otherwise have been at Alcester, Droitwich or Wall. This would account for ditched areas and hard standings. People would have come to the market and might have stayed overnight, depending on the distance they had travelled. Booths would have provided food, and this would have generated the debris on the site. Some of the pottery might even have been a commodity traded at the market. The site's function as a meeting place might also have included some sort of religious significance, although there is nothing in the finds that suggests this, and might have led to it becoming a local administrative centre. In this, it could have succeeded Metchley which presumably had local administrative functions when it housed a garrison and until it was abandoned in the second century, when occupation of the Longdales Road site begins. The prominent location of the site and the unnecessary elaboration of the ditches would make the site stand out and emphasise its status. It might even have become a hamlet or village.

A comparable site to the ditched enclosure at Longdales Road is the Roman farmstead near Shenstone, which was excavated by trenching in the 1930s. It was a double-ditched, roughly square enclosure with straight sides and rounded corners that measured 100m (330ft) by 93m (310ft) from the centre of the outer ditch, slightly larger than the Longdales Road site. The shape of the site and the V-shaped profile of its ditches suggested to its exca-vators that it had military origins and later became a farmstead, but there are no other military features and the pottery from the site indicates that it was occupied from the second to the fourth centuries. In contrast to Longdales, though, the limited excavation at Shenstone suggested that the enclosure there contained a substantial building, with dressed sandstone, roof tiles, and lead. As well as its general form and size, another similarity between it and the Longdales Road site is the occurrence of heat-shattered pebbles, which at Shenstone were found in large quantities in one of the enclosure ditches.

The farmstead at Longdales Road was a new establishment, with no Iron Age antecedents, in contrast to the Langley Mill Farm site on the M6 Toll motorway, where, adjacent to the Iron Age enclosure and stretching down from a hill crest towards a stream, there were four large roughly rectangular ditched enclosures measuring 40 to 70m across and of second to third century date *(23)*. These were presumably for livestock, although an acid soil meant that bone survival was poor, and possibly for collection of stock from several farms, as suggested above for the Longdales Road site. Some of the enclosures were joined and there were also probable ditched droveways to channel stock into them. The enclosures contained shallow pits and post holes but the only identifiable Roman structure was a small rectangular timber building with a possible hearth which could have been a stockman's or shepherd's hut. A series of small enclosures that cut across the northern part of the northernmost enclosure and continue to the north may be Roman rectilinear ditched fields or paddocks, but their date is uncertain. The site lies on what was marginal land, heathland used as rough pasture, in the medieval and post-medieval periods and up to its enclosure in the 1820s.

Pottery from these sites shows that they were part of local market networks. The ditched enclosures and paddocks at Longdales Road and Langley Mill Farm and the funnelling ditches and fenced enclosures in one phase of the Metchley fort suggest a specialisation in livestock, possibly to meet the demands of places like Droitwich, Alcester and Wall for meat, hides or fleeces. The sites are not on the best quality agricultural land, which would have been arable, but on the second best land, which we would expect to have been used for grazing. Similarly in the area around Wroxeter Roman settlements are on grazing quality land.

Extensive trenching by Cathy Mould at Peddimore, close to Wiggins Hill where a Roman settlement has been inferred from pottery found in fieldwalking, revealed no evidence for Roman activity. Probable prehistoric features near a former stream channel were separated from medieval features by alluvium. In the Roman period, the wetter part of the site could have been used for seasonal grazing, as a hay meadow, or for other managed waterside resources such as withies.

Fieldwalking in the Sutton Coldfield area has located concentrations of Roman pottery in small quantities, which would be interpreted elsewhere as evidence for manuring with domestic debris, but because they can be seen in the wider context of extensive field survey they can be recognised as significant local concentrations. As was found in the Wroxeter Hinterland study, which looked at the rural landscape around that Roman city, there seems to be relatively low use of pottery in these rural settlements with a rapid fall-off in pottery quantities with distance from the nearest town, in this case Wall. The two main concentrations, Over Green and Wiggins Hill, are just over 1km apart and each is close to a medieval farm in a medieval hamlet. It is of course possible that the Roman farm lies directly under the medieval site. If this is so, then the small quantity of pottery may be because the fieldwalking is in an area which is peripheral to the main settlement. The type of settlement probably indicated by these pottery concentrations was demonstrated by excavations at Wishaw Hall Farm just outside Birmingham. This site consisted of a square or rectangular ditched enclosure about 50m across, with a double ditch on one side, a trackway approaching it and probable field boundaries around it.

Ten sherds of Roman pottery from medieval deposits at two adjacent excavations at Moor Street and Park Street in the Bull Ring, Birmingham city centre are, like the fieldwalking finds from Sutton Coldfield, a small but locally significant quantity and hint at a farmstead here. Small quantities of Roman pottery suggesting the existence of settlements have also been found in excavations under the medieval Saracen's Head in Kings Norton and on the Northfield Relief Road not far from the line of a Roman road. The sherds from most of a single pot found by Stephanie Ratkai alongside Westhill Road in Kings Norton are difficult to interpret: do they indicate some sort of special deposit? Some of the hundreds of fragments of pottery found in the upper part of the gravels of the River Rea at Saltley towards the end of the nineteenth century (above the deposits in which the Palaeolithic hand-axe was found) were said to be Roman. The place name 'Witton' might be derived from *vicus* and therefore indicate another possible Roman settlement.

The settlement site indicated by the surface pottery concentration at Over Green lies at one corner of a rectilinear field system at the Burrells in Sutton Coldfield, much of which survives as actual field boundaries, that may be Roman or earlier in origin *(38)*. It is similar to demonstrably Roman or pre-Roman field systems elsewhere in the country. Assarting (the clearance of previously uncultivated land), which is documented here in the 1240s, is unlikely to have resulted in such a regular field system. It is more likely that the medieval assarters reused existing boundaries in land that had been abandoned after the Roman period. The alignment of the Roman road found at Swarthmore Road suggests that it may be part of land division on a square or rectangular grid.

In addition to structures and objects found in deliberate search several Roman coins have been found by chance. These are mainly single coins but there are some hoards. Some of the individual coins are types which are unlikely to have been lost in Britain during the Roman period and are therefore likely to be more recent losses. One of the hoards is from near Wiggins Hill, where a Roman settlement is suggested by a concentration of pottery, and another is from near the site at Wishaw Hall Farm described above.

BIRMINGHAM'S FIRST INDUSTRIES

The earliest evidence for industry in Birmingham consists of Roman pottery kilns at Perry Barr and Sutton Coldfield. The Perry Barr site, in Wellington Road, was discovered in 1959. It lies on red clay which was used as raw material for the pottery it produced. Although no actual kilns were found, fragments of them give us some idea of what they looked like. There were many pieces of fired clay rods ('fire bars'), which would have been laid inside

38 Field system at the Burrells in Sutton Coldfield

the kiln's oven, between the wall and a pedestal in its centre, forming a rack like the spokes of a wheel on which the pots were placed. The rods were tapered, and the presence of two sizes of rod, 37cm (15in) and 45cm to 50cm (18 to 20in) long, suggests that there were two different-sized kilns. There were also pieces of a clay floor from another type of kiln, which had holes in it to allow the hot air to circulate, and flat pieces of fired clay, probably part of the kiln's wall *(39)*. Although the excavators of the site felt that the fire bars, floor and wall fragments were the only remains of the kilns themselves, they also found what they described as well-defined shallow hollows in the clay subsoil, some with steep or even vertical sides. They interpreted these as places where clay was dug out to construct the kilns, but the hollows may have been the location of the kilns themselves. A photograph of excavation on the site shows pottery being dug out of an oval pit, which could have been the oven of a kiln. There were also some roughly cobbled surfaces.

As noted above, some of the Roman pottery found at Perry Barr dates to the late first or early second century and shows that there was some sort of settlement on the site before pottery manufacture took place on it. The debris of pottery actually produced on the site consisted of 'wasters', pieces of vessels that had been misfired causing them to distort and shatter. The kilns produced jars, bowls and handled tankards, whose form dates them to the second century, between AD 150 and 200 *(40)*. Between a quarter and a half of the wasters were from handled tankards, which had a capacity of 1.4

39 Firebars and part of the oven floor from the Roman pottery kiln at Wellington Road, Perry Barr. *Copyright Birmingham Museums and Art Gallery*

40 Roman pottery from the kiln in Wellington Road, Perry Barr. *Copyright Handsworth Historical Society*

litres (one quart). The tankards must have been used to drink a beverage like ale, cider or mead. They are particularly characteristic of the Roman pottery industries of the Severn Valley, where they were made from orange coloured clay. Although products of the Severn Valley kilns are found on Roman sites in Birmingham, the tankards may have been made locally to meet a demand for this type of vessel because those made in the Severn valley were costly and/or difficult to obtain. The handles of the Perry Barr tankards are more like those made at Roman pottery kilns in north Warwickshire than the Severn Valley products, suggesting that a potter may have moved into the area from north Warwickshire and made this preferred vessel form in local clays.

The demand for tankards locally was such that they were also made at the other Roman pottery kiln in Birmingham, at Sherifoot Lane in Sutton Coldfield, along with other vessel forms. At this site an actual kiln was found. It was discovered in the back garden of a house when the owner was digging a pit for a pond. This revealed a black deposit with many pieces of broken pottery, which the owner fortunately recognised as old rather than modern – they were actually pieces of second-century Roman pottery. Subsequent excavations by Paul Booth, David Symons and the author, revealed a kiln, its stokehole and an adjacent pit (possibly an abandoned kiln) containing waste pottery.

The kiln was aligned north-west to south-east. Its oven was on the south-east side and consisted of a roughly circular pit just under 1m across, dug about 80cm (2ft 8in) into the subsoil. A short flue, a channel whose sides were charred, linked the oven to a hollow about 2m (6ft 6in) wide and 40cm (16in) deep from which fuel would have been fed to a fire in the flue and oven *(41)*. The oven floor, on which pots were placed for firing, was supported by five pilasters of clay and brick-like blocks. During the excavation a cross-like arrangement of bricks was found above these, thought at the time to belong to a later phase of the kiln. However, Kirsty Nichol's study of the bricks found in the excavation showed that they formed an arch inside the kiln which sprang from the brick pillars found still in place, part of a floor and a pedestal. The bricks forming the arch were wedge-shaped and those forming the pedestal and floor were parallel-sided. The pedestals found still in place are thought to have supported two arches: this form is like that of first-century pottery kilns at Colchester. The arches subsequently collapsed resulting in the cross-shaped arrangement found in the excavation *(42)*. Pieces of fired clay bearing twig impressions were found. These are from a dome of clay daubed on a framework of branches and twigs which would have covered the oven.

The pottery produced at this kiln was all grey ware, and the forms included tankards, jars, bowls, dishes and lids. A vessel with holes perforated in its base, which was probably a cheese press, and a large *mortarium* or mixing bowl were probably one-offs. Part of a quern-stone was also found. This may have been used by the potter as a wheel or as a turntable. The vessel forms suggest that the kiln was in production between 150 and 200 AD. The 'bricks' used to support the oven's floor may have been reused from another kiln nearby, and in any case, the excavated kiln would not have stood alone. At both this and the Perry Barr site, there would have been other kilns, areas where the clay was allowed to weather, water-filled tanks or pits in which it was settled to remove unwanted pebbles and other impurities, the potter's workshop and possibly his dwelling, a covered area in which pots would be allowed to dry before firing, and a shelter for fuel.

Products of the Sutton Coldfield kiln have been identified at the Roman settlement at Coleshill. It and the Perry Barr kiln presumably served a local market which included Wall and farmsteads like those at Langley Mill Farm, Over Green and Wiggins Hill. Neither kiln site is on a known road line. The Perry Barr site is just under 1km from Icknield Street and the Sutton site is over 2km from Icknield Street, but the latter is less than 100m from a

41 The Roman pottery kiln in Sherifoot Lane, Sutton Coldfield, showing the circular pit which formed the base of the oven and a blackened flue joining it to the stoke-hole

medieval road line (just east of the present A5127) which follows a natural ridge *(50)* and, as suggested above, could have been in use before the Roman period.

Hollows at the Perry Barr site may be the result of clay extraction. The Sutton Coldfield kiln is on sandy subsoil and not near an obvious clay source but may have used clay contained within a glacial drift deposit. The proximity to a reliable fuel supply was probably more important. It is near Hill Wood, extensive medieval and post-medieval woodland which was managed as coppice in the medieval and post-medieval periods. If it were coppice in the Roman period as well, this would have ensured a continuing supply of the wood needed for the kiln. The Perry Barr kiln is not far from Butlers Coppice, which is shown on eighteenth-century maps.

42 Collapsed brick arches in the Roman pottery kiln at Sherifoot Lane, Sutton Coldfield

As described above, pottery was also being made at the Metchley fort. The evidence for this consists of fragments of misfired pottery, a potter's kick wheel and the fabric of the *mortaria*, and possibly the flagons.

BIRMINGHAM IN THE ROMAN EMPIRE

What effect did the Roman Empire have on the Birmingham area? There would have been an influx of people from other parts of Britain and abroad, including soldiers and their followers, administrators, merchants, craftspeople and travellers along roads, all of whom would have come into contact with the indigenous people. The Roman roads were not the first communication routes in the area but they contrasted with existing tracks, which would not have been surfaced and which would have developed though use as preferred routes rather than laid out along surveyed lines.

The roads and Metchley fort were imposed on the landscape and took up land that was already being used for something, even if only as woodland or rough grazing, and their construction affected a much larger area. The buried soil under the Roman road in Sutton Park has a podzol profile, suggesting heathland or possibly woodland in the middle of the first century. We can see from the excavated remains at Metchley fort that large quantities of timber would have been required for building its various phases, and it was presumably obtained by felling considerable numbers of standard trees in local woodland. Wattlework in the fort's buildings and fuel for its ovens and hearths could have come from woodland already managed as coppice, and the fuel for the pottery kilns is similarly likely to have been obtained from managed woodland.

Agricultural production may have increased and some specialisation may have occurred as a result of the need to supply a military garrison and incorporation into a market economy. Charred seeds of wheat, barley, peas and beans from Metchley show what crops local farmers were growing in the first century AD. The pollen evidence for woodland regeneration suggests that land may have been used less intensively in the later first century and pollen also shows that there was grass and heathland. Pollen and dung beetles in peat near the River Tame in Perry Barr indicate grassland, with grazing animals, about 330 AD. This is consistent with the indirect evidence for livestock specialisation provided by the ditched enclosures and paddocks at Longdales Road and Langley Mill Farm and by the funnelling ditches in the *vicus* and fencing in the fort itself in one of the Metchley phases. The Langley Mill Farm enclosures are on what might be regarded as land less suited to crops than to livestock but near a water supply for that stock. Agricultural products could have been sold at towns such as Droitwich, Alcester and Wall and farmers could have become dependent upon the prosperity of these places. Rural settlements obtained consumer goods like pottery from the same trading networks.

The overall settlement pattern probably consisted of separate farmsteads as it had before the Roman conquest, but the detailed relationship of the Roman to the Iron Age settlement pattern is unclear. At Longdales Road there is no evidence for an Iron Age settlement in the area excavated, and at Langley Mill Farm we do not know whether there was continuity of occupation or whether the Iron Age enclosure simply survived as an earthwork suitable for reuse. The Longdales Road site is next to a road, and we might expect new settlements to take advantage of the road network. Local potters supplied these settlements and others nearby. The contrast between the quantities of pottery on the sites in the south of the Birmingham area compared to those in the north may be a measure of the greater degree of Romanisation of the former or simply a measure of availability of pottery, particularly for those sites near to major roads.

A marked contrast between Birmingham in the Roman period and Birmingham in the Middle Ages is the lack of a focal point. No urban centre developed, nor was there, on current evidence, any sort of nucleated settlement other than the small and short-lived *vicus* at Metchley fort and possibly a group of farms at Longdales Road. Unlike other places in the country where a *vicus* ultimately developed into a medieval town, the Metchley *vicus* obviously did not become Birmingham city centre. This was because there was no previous tradition of an administrative or commercial centre such as a hillfort in the vicinity that the *vicus* could itself have succeeded, and because the location of the *vicus* had little relationship to the existing settlement pattern. The *vicus* might, though, have established or continued a practice of having a place in the area at which produce from scattered farms was collected and which acted as a market place. This practice, together with a local administrative function, may have been continued by the Longdales Road site.

THE FIFTH CENTURY AND BEYOND: BIRMINGHAM'S DARK AGES?

The only archaeological evidence for the Anglo-Saxon period in Birmingham currently consists of an iron spearhead from Edgbaston, possibly a pottery vessel found near St Nicolas's church in Kings Norton and drainage gullies at Longbridge. This does not of course mean that no-one was living in Birmingham for several centuries: most of the place names in Birmingham, including Birmingham itself, are of Anglo-Saxon origin, and charters referring to estates in Yardley and *Hellerege* in Kings Norton show that there were settlements within the area of the modern city during this period. It is difficult to say exactly where these settlements were or what they looked like. By analogy with other parts of the country, they are likely to have been individual dwellings and hamlets rather than villages until shortly before the Norman Conquest and were not necessarily on the same sites as medieval villages, but some may have been on or adjacent to sites occupied in the Roman period.

Birmingham's Roman settlements can be dated to no later than the fourth century by the pottery found on them, but the proximity of some known Roman sites, either excavated or indicated by pottery concentrations, to medieval sites still occupied today is particularly noticeable. The Roman enclosure at Longdales Road is next to Lilycroft Farm, which is mentioned in documents in 1314. The existing field boundaries, which are probably medieval, respect the Roman paddocks running at right angles to Icknield Street. The main north-south field boundary changes direction to follow the eastern side of the Roman enclosure. In the north of the city, Roman pottery has been found around the medieval hamlet at Wiggins Hill and next to a medieval moated site in the hamlet of Over Green. The same site might simply have been selected at different periods for the same reasons, such as good drainage and proximity to a water supply, which would have appealed to a farmer in the medieval period as much as to one in the Roman period. However, the close proximity does look more than coincidental and suggests that these sites may have been occupied continuously, therefore indicating the location of our elusive Anglo-Saxon sites.

By way of contrast, but at the same time emphasising the significance of the sites where continuity of occupation does seem likely, other Roman settlements and managed landscapes were abandoned during the Roman period. At Metchley, occupation of the *vicus* was short-lived and confined to the earliest period of the fort, and there is no evidence for occupation of the fort itself beyond the second century. This site might be regarded as atypical because it presumably remained in government and military control. However, other sites were also part of wider economic networks. The enclosures at Langley Mill Farm may have been abandoned by the fourth century. As noted above, they are on land that was better suited to pasture than to arable and was unenclosed common used for rough grazing until the nineteenth century. The specialisation in cattle rearing inferred from the location of the site and its structures would have been dependent on market demand. When that market no longer existed, the relatively poor soils combined with its relative isolation would have made it unattractive for continuing occupation at a subsistence level that would have required crops as well. The apparent abandonment of the Burrells field system, on good agricultural land and next to two medieval settlements that may have Roman origins, could be related to market forces and resultant changes in agricultural practices. Pollen from the Metchley Roman fort ditch indicates a transition from an open landscape to increasing woodland in the later Roman period, with some arable cultivation around the site in the Anglo-Saxon or medieval periods.

Despite popular belief, unfortunately repeated over and over again, there is no evidence that the first 'Birmingham' was at the crossing of the River Rea between Digbeth and Deritend. This was prone to flooding until relatively recent times and is unlikely to have been favoured as a settlement site. As noted in Chapters 4 and 5, excavations at Floodgate Street have shown that medieval occupation here was short-lived and that its post-medieval use was for a water-using industry. Other locations altogether have been suggested to be the site of an Anglo-Saxon settlement, such as Hockley and Broad Street to the north-west and west of the city centre. Even within the Digbeth area, the site that became the centre of the medieval town, around St Martin's church and near a spring line on the valley side, would have been more attractive for settlement than the river crossing. As noted above, Roman pottery from Moor Street and Park Street suggests that there was a Roman settlement of some sort here. Although there is apparently no archaeological evidence for Anglo-Saxon Birmingham in the Bull Ring area other than one or two fragments of pottery, a hitherto neglected site deserves closer consideration.

The curious Parsonage Moat shown on eighteenth-century maps near the moated manor house may provide some evidence. At that time it surrounded the home of the incumbent of St Martin's, and it is possible that it was originally built in the medieval period for that purpose: there was a moated rectory near the church at Northfield, and another in Tipton just outside Birmingham. The status the moat gave to the site would however make it conflict and possibly compete with the adjoining moated manor house. It has also been suggested that it was a 'home farm' for the lord of the manor, separating the centre of agricultural operations from his residence. This situation occurs at other places in the country, and suggests that this part of Birmingham had a rural rather than urban appearance in the twelfth century, just before its rapid growth and transformation into a town. It could also have been the first manor house, established in the twelfth century and replaced soon after by the manor house with its large circular moat. However, another possible interpretation is suggested by the location, size and shape of Parsonage Moat, but this must be based on the site as we see it on historic maps, for no trace of it was found in excavations and observations in Edgbaston Street and Wrottesley Street respectively, and the rest of it now lies under Pershore Street, which was constructed in the nineteenth century. The site is opposite the junction of the original road from Dudley with Edgbaston Street, which runs to St Martin's church and the market place at the Bull Ring, and close to Lady Well. On maps of 1750 and 1808, Parsonage Moat is a square or rectangular moat about 50m across (43). These dimensions are very similar to those of a ninth-century manorial site at Goltho in Lincolnshire which consisted of a roughly rectangular ditched area about 48m across which contained timber buildings. Was Parsonage Moat similarly a late Saxon manor which stood in isolation but formed a focus for the centre of the medieval town established in the twelfth century?

Steven Bassett has suggested that there was a church predating St Martins on the site occupied by the medieval priory or hospital, 500m to the north, but the arguments he puts forward in support of this are unconvincing. However, the shape of the graveyard around St Martin's itself hints at the existence

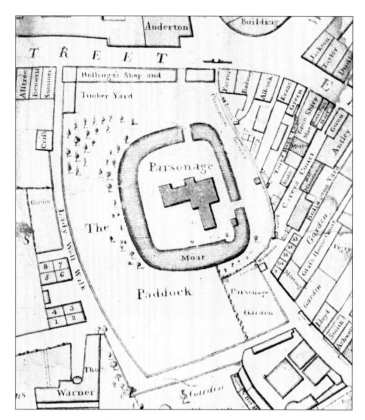

43 Parsonage Moat
on Sheriff's map of
1808

of a church on this site before the twelfth century. Although it had already
been encroached upon by buildings by the time it is depicted on eighteenth-
century maps *(45)*, the outer line of these buildings on the north, east and
south sides is curvilinear, hinting at a circular churchyard of the type associated
with churches founded in western Britain and the Welsh Marches before the
Norman Conquest. Such a church could have served a scattered community
and does not necessarily indicate a village. It would, though, like the suggested
late Saxon manor, have provided a focus for the new medieval town.

Any discussion of Anglo-Saxon Birmingham is inevitably largely specu-
lative because of the sparseness of information. From the twelfth century
onwards, however, we have a wide range of archaeological evidence.

CHAPTER 4

MEDIEVAL BIRMINGHAM: TOWN AND COUNTRY, INDUSTRY AND AGRICULTURE

Although it could be said that the medieval period in the country as a whole begins with the Norman Conquest of 1066, the archaeological record for medieval Birmingham begins in the twelfth century. This period marks the creation of the town of Birmingham and its establishment as a commercial and industrial centre within the region, together with increasing exploitation of the landscape around it.

The Middle Ages is the earliest time from which we can build up a picture of the general appearance of the whole of the area of the present city with some confidence. Our picture is put together from a combination of documentary evidence and a wide range of archaeological material, which includes surviving buildings and earthworks as well as excavated remains. The archaeological evidence for this period relates to different types of settlements, individual houses and other buildings and structures, roads and tracks, the acquisition and use of pottery and other objects, fuels, agriculture and other rural land use, and trade and industry *(44)*.

There are several parish churches of medieval origin and timber-framed buildings. These include cruck-framed buildings and barns, some of which have been dated by dendrochronology (tree-ring dating). This has also indicated re-use of timbers, for example at Monyhull Hall barn. Earthwork remains include house platforms, moated sites, fishpond dams, deer park boundaries and ridge and furrow. Excavations which have investigated or located medieval remains have taken place in the Bull Ring, Digbeth and Deritend areas of the city centre, in Sutton Coldfield town centre, in the village centre at Kings Norton, in the hamlet of Minworth Greaves, on some

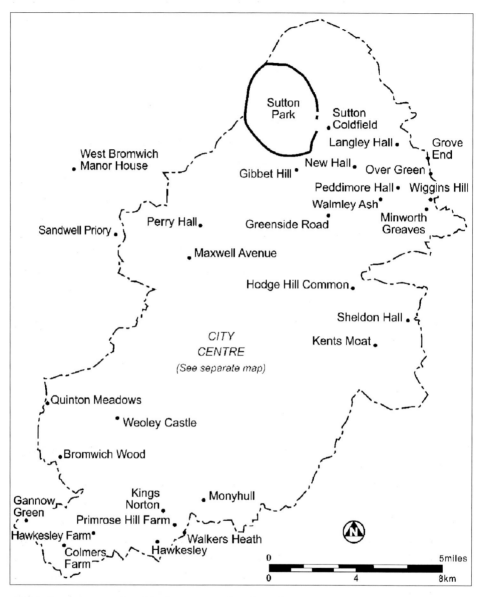

Sutton
Park

Sutton
• Coldfield

Langley Hall •   • Grove
•   End

West Bromwich   New Hall •   Over Green •
• Manor House   Gibbet Hill •   Peddimore Hall • Wiggins Hill
                                     Walmley Ash•
                                                    Minworth
Sandwell Priory •   Perry Hall •   Greenside Road• Greaves

                  • Maxwell Avenue

                     Hodge Hill Common•

                                    Sheldon Hall •

              CITY   Kents Moat •
              CENTRE
           (See separate map)

        • Quinton Meadows

              • Weoley Castle

         • Bromwich Wood

              Kings   • Monyhull
Gannow   Norton•
Green   Primrose Hill Farm•
Hawkesley Farm•
        • Colmers   • Walkers Heath
          Farm   Hawkesley

        0   5miles
        0   4   8km

44 Medieval sites mentioned in the text. *Based on the Ordnance Survey map and reproduced by permission of Ordnance Survey on behalf of the Controller of Her Majesty's Stationery Office, © Crown Copyright 100042011*

of the moated sites and in the fields around Peddimore. Plant and insect remains providing evidence for the surrounding environment have been found on the city centre sites, and some of these have also yielded debris from industrial processes. Beyond the city centre, pollen has been recovered at Gannow Green moat. In addition to excavated finds, medieval pottery has been found in fieldwalking in the Sutton Coldfield area.

Archaeological evidence, discussed below, suggests that the town of Birmingham was a new creation of the twelfth century. Before that, there was no town or village on its site, although there may have been scattered farmsteads in its vicinity. The only earlier settlements were the possible Roman farmstead and the possible Saxon manor described in the previous chapter. By contrast, the medieval settlements at Lilycroft Farm in Kings Norton and Over Green and Wiggins Hill in Sutton Coldfield may be on sites continuously occupied from the Roman period, judging from the proximity of Roman features or Roman pottery. Roman pottery has also been found in Kings Norton village and at the moated site at Maxwell Avenue in Handsworth. At other medieval sites, however, no Roman material has been found, suggesting they were, like Birmingham itself, new settlements, albeit possibly near to sites that had been occupied earlier. No Roman pottery was found in excavations at Weoley Castle, Kents Moat, Hawkesley Farm Moat or Gannow Green, or in excavations or fieldwalking around Peddimore Hall.

BIRMINGHAM NEW TOWN:
A MEDIEVAL MARKET AND INDUSTRIAL TOWN

The medieval town of Birmingham, newly established in the twelfth century, consisted of a moated manor house, parish church and what may have been the original market place in the area between them. There was a large triangular market place in front of the church, a row of houses to the north in 'burgage plots' whose divisions can still be seen, a deer park to the east, and a wet area to the south in which there were water-using industries such as leather tanning. A causeway may have been built over wet ground to a crossing of the River Rea at the same time, encouraging some people to live at this entry point to the new town. The success of the market and no doubt active encouragement of the industries led to a subsequent planned expansion of the town including the addition of new streets, the construction of more houses to the west and south, and the establishment of a priory or hospital *(45, 46)*.

If, as suggested below, the moated manor house was a ringwork with an outer enclosure, then with the parish church outside it and a market place and High Street beyond, the new town looks very much like one of the small medieval planned towns in the Welsh Marches such as Kilpeck or Richards Castle. The resemblance would be even greater if like these it were defended.

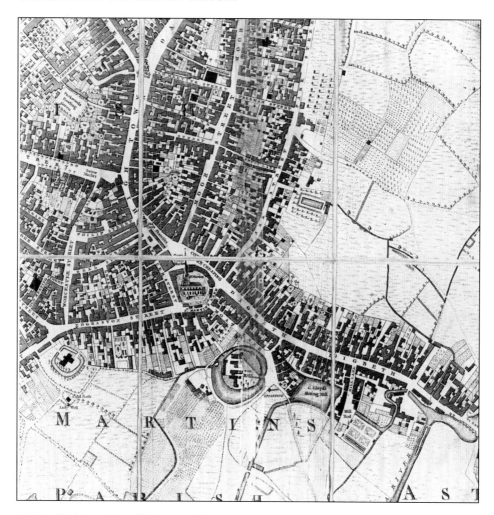

45 Detail of Samuel Bradford's map of 1750 showing the St Martin's, Digbeth and Deritend area

The large ditch found in excavation, as described below, to the north-east of the church and manor house and interpreted as the boundary between the town and deer park could have been a town ditch, which might have extended as far north as the junction of High Street and New Street, then south to Parsonage Moat. The rest of the boundary would be formed by the water-course joining the two moats. This would explain the name Hersum (lord's or lordship) Ditch given to a boundary on this line in the fourteenth century and would mean that the manor house was near the entrance to the enclosed area from Digbeth, the road to Dudley was at an entrance on the west, and New Street was at the northern corner of the enclosure, where it was entered from High Street. This would also explain the location of New Street: a road heading for the northern entrance into the enclosure and widening to form an additional market place just outside it.

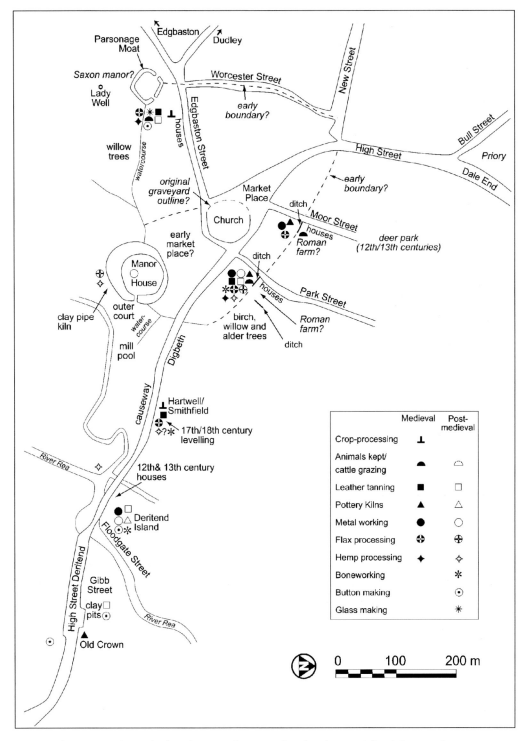

46 The St Martin's, Digbeth and Deritend area: medieval and post medieval features. Streets, watercourses and moats are as shown on Samuel Bradford's map of 1750, and details from excavations are shown schematically

The new town was close to the boundary between what may have been two large parishes, Harborne and Aston. In local terms, it lay between three possible earlier sites. The Roman settlement indicated by the pottery from excavations at Moor Street and Park Street could have been a ditched farmstead which might have still been visible as earthworks in the twelfth century, whenever it was abandoned. Similarly, even if the putative Saxon manor at Parsonage Moat was out of use by the twelfth century, the moat itself was visible. I have suggested in the previous chapter that the curvilinear shape of St Martin's churchyard may indicate an early church site here, and Steven Bassett has suggested on the basis of burials observed in the eighteenth century that the Priory or Hospital of St Thomas, discussed below, was founded at what was previously a church serving Birmingham.

The availability of several resources in close proximity probably played a part in the location of Birmingham new town. Several streams and a spring line provided water for domestic and industrial purposes. The location of the manor house may have been determined by preceding features like the church but its position took advantage of the water supply. The church, market place and houses were on a slightly higher, dryer site but had access to water nearby. The plant and animal remains from excavations show how heath and woodland were being exploited. The botanical evidence suggests that there may have been substantial woodland in the twelfth and thirteenth centuries, which would have been important not only as a building material but perhaps even more significantly as a source of fuel. It could also have been part of wood pasture, land managed for both woodland and grazing. Clay was also readily available for use in daub, which was applied on wattles filling the panels of timber-framed buildings, and for the manufacture of pottery and tiles.

THE PARISH CHURCH

St Martin's church was in existence by the thirteenth century but its almost total rebuilding in the nineteenth century left only the footings of the tower of the medieval church and a fragment of its wall. However, fragments of stone found during the nineteenth-century restoration are said to have included pieces with a chevron decoration that are likely to be of twelfth-century date. The surrounding graveyard was used until the nineteenth century and the consequent density and elaboration of burials, as revealed in Richard Cherrington's excavation of its northern part in 2001, meant that no intact interments survived which were datable to earlier than the eighteenth century. Disarticulated bones and fragments of bone in later graves or in charnel pits were all that was left of the many medieval burials that must have taken place here. Just outside the church to the west, a medieval stone lined well is likely to have been for public use.

The churchyard of St Martin's was not the only place in which the dead were buried in the medieval town. The Priory or Hospital of St Thomas had its own graveyard, and an unexpected discovery in the excavations in Park Street was that of two thirteenth-century graves, on land which was either still part of the deer park at the time or in the backyard of one of the properties on the newly created Park Street. These people may have been buried here, rather than in the graveyard of St Martin's church only 100m away, because they were criminals and therefore could not be buried in consecrated ground, or because they were the victims of foul play or disease and had to be secretly buried.

THE MANOR HOUSE (BIRMINGHAM MOAT)

The moat originally surrounding the medieval manor house is shown on eighteenth-century maps as wide and circular, with an entrance gap on its eastern side, but its width by this time might have resulted from repeated cleaning and erosion of its sides. It remained open until 1816. The circular form of the moat suggests that it was a ringwork (a type of castle in which the buildings were surrounded by a circular ditch, bank and fence), which is likely to be twelfth century in date, and stonework from the site, discussed below, also suggests a twelfth-century origin. A ringwork would be consistent with the *castrum* mentioned in a charter of 1166 which gives the lord of the manor, Peter de Birmingham, the right to hold a market.

The south-west and south-east parts of the moat and the area enclosed by it were investigated in far from ideal conditions by Lorna Watts during the construction of the Wholesale Markets on part of the site between 1973 and 1975. The north-west part of the moat was observed and recorded in controlled conditions by Chris Patrick during the construction of a new road in 2000.

Lorna Watts observed a single wall of mortared sandstone blocks just inside the moat on the south-east side. The wall had been incorporated into a later structure, which was faced with well-cut ashlar blocks and had a chamfered plinth *(47)*. The south side of this structure was about 11m long with a return wall at least 4m long, and it had a buttress about 4m from its south-east corner, possibly relating to a bay of the building. The structure could be the end wall of a building, the base of a stair, an oriel window, or a tower. It has been dated to the thirteenth century from the form of the buttress. Stones found near it include a piece with a moulding, possibly from a door jamb, in a form which was used at other sites nearby such as Sandwell Priory. This form is twelfth century in date and may have been part of the building represented by the earlier wall. The only other feature observed was a line of stakes on the inner part of the north side of the entrance gap on the east side of the moat. The medieval pottery recovered by Watts is predominantly of thirteenth to

47 Stone walls of the manor house exposed during the construction of the Wholesale Markets. The dressed face of the earlier wall is visible behind the chamfered face. *Copyright Birmingham Museums and Art Gallery*

fourteenth century date. Metalwork and pottery found when the earlier Wholesale Markets were constructed in 1883 included a fifteenth-century Spanish vessel, a spur, knife blades, and sheep bones with grooves in them that may have been used to sharpen pins.

Clay floor tiles and roof tiles, some of them glazed, were found but they were not in deposits that could be dated to the medieval period. Similarly, deposits containing coal at the manor house site were assumed to be post-medieval in date but, as noted below, roof tiles and coal have been found in thirteenth-century deposits on other sites in the city centre.

Chris Patrick recorded a cross section through the moat, which showed that it survived to a depth of 2.5m. Although the bulk of the infill was nineteenth century in date, the lowest layers contained a rim of a cooking pot of twelfth- or thirteenth-century date, and organic material which included heather seeds and pollen from a range of tree species and hemp or hops. This corresponds with the evidence for heather in medieval deposits on other nearby sites, where it would have been used for roofing or animal bedding, and for hemp seeds in late medieval and early post-medieval deposits. The observations also demonstrated the accuracy of William Westley's 1731 map despite its rather sketchy appearance, since Samuel Bradford's neater map of 1750 does not show the moat extending this far north.

The rather meagre archaeological evidence from Birmingham's manor house therefore suggests that it was first built in the twelfth century as a ringwork which contained a stone building with moulded stonework. This was replaced by another stone building in the thirteenth century. In the twelfth and thirteenth centuries Birmingham manor house would have looked similar to Weoley Castle at the same time, and consisted of stone and timber buildings surrounded by a moat accompanied by a bank and timber fence.

A sixteenth-century document mentions an outer court to the south-east of the manor house. There was also an outer court at Weoley Castle, discussed below, and at both sites it is likely to have been a ditched and fenced enclosure. There could also have been another outer court to the north of the manor house, between the moat and the churchyard, and the market may have been held in it.

THE DEER PARK

A ditch found in Cathy Mould's and Bob Burrows' excavations in Moor Street and Park Street in 2000 and 2001 respectively is interpreted as the boundary of the deer park. It was up to 7m wide and up to 2m deep and was presumably accompanied by a bank and fence but no evidence for these survived *(48)*. The excavations showed that it had been filled in by the early fourteenth century. Botanical evidence showed that it was wet, and it was probably dug at least

48 Excavation of the large boundary ditch at Park Street. The ditch runs from left to right across the photograph and the archaeologist is in its base partly along the line of an existing natural watercourse. From analysis of property records, George Demidowicz has shown that its line was followed by a boundary feature known from 1341 to 1681 as Hersum or Hassams ditch. A similarly-named feature in Coventry also formed the boundary between a deer park and house plots, and the name may mean 'lordship' or 'jurisdiction'. As suggested above, it may have originated as a boundary line around the new town.

THE GROWTH OF THE TOWN

Twelfth-century pottery has been found in a pit on the Edgbaston Street frontage and in Moor Street and Park Street. This might be expected at the centre of the town, near St Martin's church and the manor house, but more surprising is the evidence for thirteenth- and possibly twelfth-century occupation at Floodgate Street, on Deritend Island between two channels of the River Rea. A ditch along the High Street frontage of this site may have resulted from the construction of a causeway up to a bridge over the river. It was followed by two phases of ditches forming property boundaries. The main boundary ran north–south at right angles to the main road and there were subdividing ditches running east–west. The houses would have been on the street frontage and no trace of them survived, but their occupants had thrown their broken pottery into the ditches. This pottery included very little of the white or buff-coloured pottery, probably made in south Staffordshire or north Warwickshire, which is fairly common on Birmingham sites from the middle of the thirteenth century into the fourteenth, suggesting that occupation had ceased by 1300 and possibly by about 1250.

Perhaps the Floodgate Street site was abandoned by its occupants because continual flooding from the river became intolerable. It might however have been occupied when better land was not available, and its occupants might have taken advantage of the planned expansion of the town to the north of St Martin's church onto land which had formerly been part of the deer park. As noted above, the large ditch found at Park Street and Moor Street was infilled in the late thirteenth or early fourteenth centuries and these two streets were laid out over it. At Park Street, a ditch running parallel with the new street formed the boundary of land attached to a house on its frontage. Further down the valley slope the thirteenth- or early fourteenth-century pits discovered at Hartwell Smithfield Garage were probably behind dwellings of this date, and on the other side of the River Rea at Gibb Street and Heath Mill Lane there were pits, post holes, a gully and layers containing thirteenth- and fourteenth-century pottery.

After this initial success there may have been a reduction in the intensity of activity, as has been observed in other towns in the West Midlands and other parts of the country. No late fourteenth to early sixteenth-century pottery was found at either Gibb Street or Hartwell Smithfield Garage and there is relatively little pottery of this date range from the Bull Ring sites. However, the small quantities of pottery do not necessarily indicate abandonment or reduction in the intensity of activity. Greater use may have been made of metal vessels for cooking (an iron cauldron was found at Edgbaston Street) and there may have been changes in methods of rubbish disposal. Rather than being dumped near a dwelling, domestic refuse, which would include broken pottery as well as organic waste, might have been thrown onto a midden, and taken off the site to spread over fields. Medieval pottery on field surfaces in the Sutton Coldfield area shows that this is what happened in rural areas.

In contrast with the other excavated sites, late fifteenth- or early sixteenth-century pottery has been found at Floodgate Street next to the River Rea, showing renewed activity here after abandonment in the thirteenth century. This may have been industrial rather than domestic, attracted by the water supply, but might also be part of a change in the form of the town, from a tight focus in the St Martin's area to development along the main roads leading to it, including Digbeth and High Street Deritend, and possibly also New Street. Whatever was happening in the town centre at this time, architectural details and dendrochronology show that new buildings were being constructed in the surrounding rural area in the fifteenth century, such as Primrose Hill Farm in Kings Norton and the barn at Minworth Greaves.

THE PRIORY OR HOSPITAL OF ST THOMAS

The archaeological evidence for St Thomas's Priory or Hospital, which existed by 1286, consists of a single piece of sandstone now in Birmingham City Museum and a photograph of stone foundations exposed in April 1898 during alterations to the Minories, north of Bull Street (5). Foundations of some of its buildings are said to have been visible in the cellars of eighteenth-century buildings. Human remains found around it during later development, such as in Upper Minories and Corporation Street, indicate the extent of its graveyard. The discovery of human bones in the late eighteenth century to the south-west of Bull Street, outside the likely extent of the Priory's precinct, is recorded by William Hutton, who says that he doubts, although unfortunately without giving his reasons, that they were in the Priory's graveyard. Despite the lack of any other information about these bones or the circumstances of their discovery, Steven Bassett has suggested that they indicate a graveyard which predated the priory, and therefore an earlier church, the predecessor of St Martin's in Birmingham new town. This is unconvincing as it fails to take into account the possibility that they were actually much older than the priory, possibly Roman or prehistoric, or post-dated it, or not even human at all. Perhaps Hutton was doubtful because the condition of the bones suggested one of these possibilities to him. If they were actually medieval human remains, they might have been derived from the priory's graveyard during earthmoving and would therefore be disarticulated, or they might have been burials made away from a graveyard for whatever reason, like those at Park Street.

LIVING AND WORKING IN MEDIEVAL BIRMINGHAM

Although no actual houses have been found, structures in what would have been their backyards, together with pottery and other objects and animal bones and plant remains tell us something about daily life in the medieval town. People were cooking food, processing crops and keeping livestock. Industries included metalworking, pottery making, leather tanning, probably bone and horn working, tile making and textile processing. The archaeological evidence paints a picture of houses and industry cheek by jowl in the medieval town of Birmingham, rather like Digbeth and Deritend as shown on nineteenth-century Ordnance Survey maps in which courts of back-to-back houses alternate with workshops. Metalworking and pottery manufacture both created a fire risk and a lot of smoke, and leather tanning was a particularly smelly process. All of these were taking in or close to the town centre. People were certainly less sensitive to these smells than we would be today, but they may also have tolerated them because they recognised the important contribution they made to the town's prosperity.

Excavations at Edgbaston Street revealed a thirteenth-century clay-lined oven with a floor of roof tiles and a pit that was probably a water tank. There was also a channel opening into a hollow, which may have been a kiln for drying or malting grain. A similar structure, but of fifteenth- or sixteenth-century date, was found at Park Street. Charred cereal grains from the infill of the large boundary ditch described above included wheat, barley, oats and rye. Burnt seeds of vetch and dock in the pits at Hartwell Smithfield Garage might have been waste from crop processing. Flax seeds found at several sites may have been eaten, if this plant was not brought here to make linen.

Linen, rope and canvas manufacture is indicated by seeds and pollen of hemp and flax at Park Street and other sites. Their fibres would have been retted or broken down by immersion in one of several watercourses. A pit at Hartwell Smithfield Garage also contained a bundle of fibres, possibly indicating textile manufacture here as well. The watercourse joining the Parsonage and the manor house moats contained dung beetles and weevils, showing that cattle were grazing nearby. Pollen and seeds indicated disturbed grassland. Animals were also kept at Moor Street and Park Street where seeds and pollen found in the park boundary ditch suggest animal fodder. There was also heather and bracken, which could have been animal bedding. A clay-lined hollow at Park Street, which was in use in the fifteenth or sixteenth centuries, may have been a pond for cattle to drink from.

The raw material for Birmingham's leather tanning industry came from the town's thriving cattle market. Leather tanning took place at Edgbaston Street and other sites in the Middle Ages. At Edgbaston Street there were several pits, some of which were lined with clay or timber to retain water. These would have contained tanning liquor, made from crushed oak bark and water, in which hides were soaked. The earliest of these went out of use and were filled with rubbish in the thirteenth century, but they were replaced by more pits and tanning continued on this site until the eighteenth century, as described below. The pits contained bark scleroids and bark beetles, which would have lived in the bark used in the tanning process, and a circular piece of bone which was probably used to scrape hides. Clay-lined pits found at Park Street may have been used for tanning: the bony cores of cattle horns and foot bones at Park Street are particularly characteristic of leather tanning waste. A piece of worked bone at Hartwell Smithfield Garage indicates another industry using animal products as a raw material, and horn would have been made into handles and other items.

Large quantities of tree pollen might have resulted from the use of wood products, such as bark for leather tanning. However, buds, seeds and cones from birch, alder and willow in the park boundary ditch at Park Street and an actual tree bole on the south side of the watercourse at Edgbaston Street indicate trees or woodland. Shoots of willow and alder, which could also have grown there in the wet area near the moats, would have been soaked in osier pits like those shown on eighteenth-century maps to make them supple for use in wattle and daub walls of timber framed buildings, and as fence panels, as linings or covers for pits, and for making baskets.

At Park Street there was smithing slag from ironworking, and smithing hearth bottoms containing coal, which was the fuel used for this process. At Moor Street, a fragment of a crucible, hammerscale and coal and charcoal were found in the park boundary ditch and in pits dug into it after it was filled in. Slag dating to the fifteenth or early sixteenth century was also found at Floodgate Street. Coal in a thirteenth-century ditch at Floodgate Street and a thirteenth- or fourteenth-century pit at Hartwell Smithfield Garage was not found with any slag or other metalworking debris and was probably being used as a domestic fuel.

Although pottery from a variety of sources – south Staffordshire, Worcester, Coventry, Buckinghamshire and even maiolica from the Mediterranean – was used in the medieval town, pottery was also made in Birmingham itself in the thirteenth and possibly twelfth centuries. It consisted mainly of jugs, possibly copying those made in the London area at the time, and cooking pots, with small quantities of bowls and dripping trays. Although no actual kilns have yet been found, their locations are indicated by 'wasters', pottery which has been over- or under-fired and has been discarded near the kiln. Birmingham's medieval pottery industry first came to light in 1953 when Robert Sherlock

49 Fragments of Deritend Ware pottery from the Old Crown, with the distinctive white clay decoration

found misfired fragments of jugs and cooking pots on the south side of High Street Deritend in his observations during road widening, and the particular style of pottery was subsequently christened Deritend Ware. In 1994, Cathy Mould's trenching to the rear of the Old Crown revealed large quantities of medieval pottery. The variable firing of the pieces and the absence of other refuse suggests that they were debris from manufacture. Virtually all of the pieces were from jugs in an orange-coloured clay decorated with lines of white clay *(64, 49)*. White clay strips on some vessels were stamped with a roller, and other decoration included applied faces and applied scales. This seems to be imitating north French decorative styles of around 1300. The orange clay is from the Mercia Mudstone which underlies this part of the city centre and would have been obtained on or close to the site itself, while the white clay used for the decoration was brought in from further afield. On the other side of Heath Mill Lane from the Old Crown, pits dug to extract clay were back-filled in the late seventeenth or eighteenth century. The potter on the Old Crown site could have been getting his clay from the same location.

Discoveries of waste pieces show that the same type of pottery was being manufactured at several locations stretching from High Street Deritend up to Moor Street. Small quantities have been found at Gibb Street, Hartwell Smithfield Garage and Moor Street. Larger quantities and one of the fired clay bars on which vessels were supported in a kiln were found in the deer park boundary ditch at Park Street. The kilns were probably in the back yards of houses, although they may have been within the deer park itself. Roof tiles were almost certainly made locally but no remains of their manufacture have yet been found.

SUTTON COLDFIELD

The historic centre of modern Birmingham's other medieval town is the parish church, Holy Trinity, situated at the junction of roads to Lichfield and Tamworth (High Street), Coleshill and Birmingham (Mill Street), across the valley of the Plants Brook to the south *(50)*. The earliest surviving parts of the church, the plinths of the tower and east end, are probably thirteenth century in origin. A house in Coleshill Street, despite its nineteenth-century brick frontage, is a timber-framed medieval hall house with a surviving timber-framed smokehood and other medieval structures may well survive behind eighteenth- and nineteenth-century frontages in Coleshill Street and High Street.

In contrast to Birmingham city centre, relatively little excavation has taken place in Sutton Coldfield. A thirteenth- or fourteenth-century oven was found in Dan Garner's excavations in Coleshill Street just opposite the church in what would have been the back yard of a house on the street frontage. The oven was oval, about 1.2m across, and was constructed in a hollow by building up a clay wall into a dome on a framework of twigs. The clay was hardened by firing. The remains consisted of the base of the oven and the adjoining hole where a fire would have been made. The oven had collapsed but still contained charred grain, mainly rye, which may be from waste or a spoilt crop used as fuel to heat an oven used for bread making, or may indicate that the oven was used for drying grain. A stone footing for the timber wall of a medieval building, possibly a kitchen, was also found in Coleshill Street. The only other excavation in Sutton Coldfield town centre which revealed probable medieval features was that by Alex Jones at Mill Street, which revealed post holes earlier than stone wall footings of seventeenth- or eighteenth-century date.

At Coleshill Street the accumulation of cultivation soils just behind the street frontage and an absence of features such as pits or any industrial debris gives medieval Sutton Coldfield a rural feel in contrast to the urban landscape of medieval Birmingham with its busy backplots. Unlike Birmingham, there was no pressure to spread beyond the street frontages into land previously unoccupied.

Sutton Coldfield's medieval manor house was on a hill on the other side of the valley from the church, and relates more to the deer park to the west, discussed below, than to the town centre. Local historian Agnes Bracken, writing in 1860, said that the buildings of the manor house were then 'still perfectly traceable' and occupied an oval area about 100 yards across within

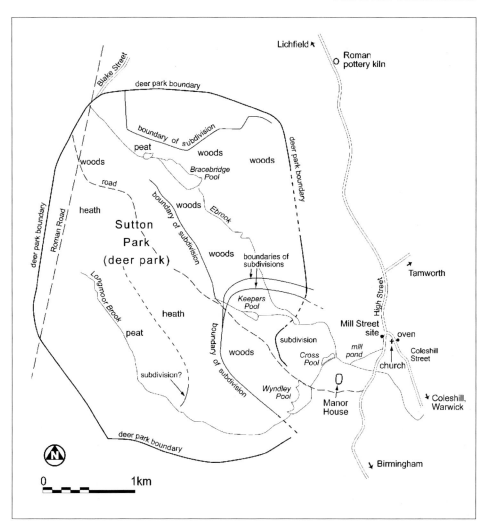

50 Medieval Sutton Coldfield and Sutton Park

which traces of buildings could be made out. Far fewer remains are now visible. They consist of the stone footings of a nineteenth-century house now occupying part of the site, large stones which were exposed in a service trench and may be from its boundary wall, decorated floor tiles and carved stones now elsewhere. The floor tiles are all inlaid, and thirteenth or fourteenth century in date. They may well be from the floor of the chapel dedicated to St Blaise which is known from documentary evidence to have existed within the manor house. The stones, also reputed to be from the chapel, include two fragments of what may have been a frieze, with the heads of two figures against a colonnade of plain columns with a zigzag upper edge *(51)*. The columns and zigzag suggest twelfth-century architectural details, therefore the stones

51 A stone head from the chapel of Sutton Coldfield manor house

and the chapel itself may also be of this date. These two stones were once set in the gable of a house, now demolished, then in Holy Trinity churchyard. Midgley's photograph of 1904 shows them accompanied by other figure and animal carvings. Other stones from the chapel, which were used to build Water Orton Bridge in the sixteenth century, include one with a large angel carved in relief and another with a smaller angel.

BIRMINGHAM'S MEDIEVAL VILLAGES, HAMLETS AND FARMS

The growth of the town of Birmingham as an industrial and market centre would have encouraged rural prosperity, in the production of food for the townspeople and plant and animal raw materials for its industries.

King's Norton

The most substantial archaeological evidence for the medieval villages that are now Birmingham's suburbs is from King's Norton and consists of surviving buildings and excavated remains. St Nicolas's church, on one side of a triangular green, is a fine late medieval church which is mainly fourteenth and fifteenth century in date but also contains twelfth-and thirteenth-century architectural features. Next to the churchyard there is a fifteenth-century timber-framed building, the Saracen's Head, and on the other side of the green remains of another medieval timber building of probable late fifteenth-century date survive behind a later frontage. A further late medieval timber-framed building survived into the 1930s, and a sandstone footing of another was excavated in 1985. Laurence Jones's excavations in 1992 on this side of the green revealed remains of timber-framed buildings and less substantial structures of thirteenth- and fourteenth-century date. The earliest structure was probably C-shaped, its open side facing the green. Its walls were constructed on horizontal beams recessed into the ground surface. This building was dismantled and the site lay empty for a while before a small structure based on vertical posts set into the ground, possibly a shed, was built in the fourteenth century. This in turn was dismantled and replaced by another building alongside the green. Two of its walls were based on horizontal beams laid in trenches with clay bases and its other walls were formed around posts on clay bases. Further posts might have indicated fences outside the building. This building was abandoned before the end of the fourteenth century and the site then appears to have become a garden. Pottery found on the site includes vessels made in Dudley, north Warwickshire and Buckinghamshire.

Excavations at the Saracen's Head have revealed a twelfth century boundary ditch and postholes of thirteenth century timber buildings under the north range and in the courtyard. As on the other side of The Green, the site seems to have subsequently lain empty until construction of the existing building, dated by dendrochronology to 1492. The excavation also revealed remains of a fifteenth-century tiled floor.

Minworth Greaves

The hamlet of Minworth Greaves, on the other side of the city, now consists of a single eighteenth-century brick farmhouse, Minworth Greaves Farm, with an adjoining timber-framed barn whose construction has been dated by dendrochronology to the fifteenth century *(52)*. William Dugdale, writing in 1656, said that it then consisted of seven houses, one of them in ruins. The hamlet formerly also contained a cruck-framed building, which has now been moved to Bournville. This has not been dated by dendrochronology but is probably of a similar date to the Smithy in Maney and New Shipton Farm, i.e. mid-fifteenth century. Katie Pack's observation of ground clearance for new development around Minworth Greaves Farm revealed ditches forming rectangular areas 18m wide, presumably bounding paddocks, behind the farmhouse and between it and ridge and furrow. The ridges, now levelled, corresponded to strip divisions of a medieval open field which are marked on a map of 1789. The ditches are dated to the thirteenth to fourteenth centuries by pottery in them. There was also a pit containing much pottery of the same date, the refuse of the inhabitants of an earlier farm on the same site. All of the pottery was from local sources and it included jugs, bowls which had been used for cooking, and cooking pots. Together, the archaeological evidence

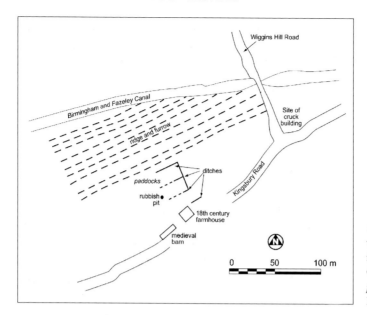

52 Buildings, earthworks and excavated features at Minworth Greaves. *Compiled from plans by the author and L-P Archaeology*

provided by the surviving building, earthworks, excavated features and pottery at Minworth Greaves presents a microcosm of Birmingham's medieval rural landscape: a farmhouse with a barn and paddocks next to it, and cultivated fields beyond.

The medieval pottery types found in excavation at Minworth Greaves are similar to those found in fieldwalking in the Sutton Coldfield area and are therefore likely to represent the pottery in everyday use by the farmers of Birmingham's medieval countryside. Jugs, bowls and jars or cooking pots were made from a white or buff-coloured clay, probably in south Staffordshire or north Warwickshire. Some of the vessels have a patchy green glaze. In addition there are cooking pots made from orange or brown clay, again a local product.

Wiggins Hill, Over Green and Grove End

A short distance away from Minworth Greaves, Wiggins Hill originally included a medieval timber-framed building and medieval pottery has been found in the fields around it. The sandstone footings of Wiggins Hill Farm, a seventeenth-century brick building, are weathered and may be reused from an earlier building on the site, which is likely to have been timber-framed and resting on a sandstone plinth. A hollow on the north side of the farmhouse is probably the quarry they came from: Wiggins Hill is on an outcrop of sandstone within Mercia Mudstone. Further north, two hamlets, Over Green and Grove End, are also on outcrops of the same material and they straddle the boundary with the parish of Wishaw in Warwickshire. Over Green includes a moated site and excavations at Pool Hall revealed stone wall footings of medieval date. Hermitage Farm, the early nineteenth-century brick building now occupying the moated site, contains worn sandstone blocks in its walls and footings which may, like those at Wiggins Hill, be from an earlier building on the site. At Grove End a cruck-framed building survives, and there are platforms indicating the location of former houses.

Farmhouses and other buildings

In addition to towns, villages and hamlets, the area of the present city contained several isolated farmsteads and other dwellings in the medieval period, some of which were surrounded by moats and are discussed below. Primrose Hill Farm (originally Hole Farm) in King's Norton is a fifteenth-century timber-framed building consisting of a hall with a cross-wing running at right-angles to its west end *(53)*. Mary Duncan's excavation to the east of the hall revealed a stone sill wall constructed of large sandstone blocks, which was cut through by a large ditch between the mid-sixteenth and seventeenth centuries. The sill could have been the base for a former timber cross-wing to the house matching that at the other end, resulting in a C-plan. Dendrochronology provided a fifteenth-century date for timbers reused in the roof of a barn at Monyhull Hall, possibly in the early seventeenth century when the hall was rebuilt.

A rectangular flat-topped mound 13m long and 9m wide alongside Coleshill Road on Hodge Hill Common, which was interpreted in the nineteenth century as a barrow, is more likely to be a house platform, probably

53 Primrose Hill Farm. The excavation in the foreground revealed remains of a cross-wing matching that at the other end of the building

medieval in date and the result of encroachment on the common *(54)*. The oval structure discovered during house construction at Greenside Road in Erdington in 1960 measured about 4.5m by 3m (15ft by 10ft) and had a clay floor, a central post and outer walls defined by a double row of post holes, the outermost posts larger than the inner. There was a gully outside the wall and there was medieval pottery on the clay floor. The structure was cut by a seventeenth-century ditch. It was interpreted by its excavator as an oval timber hut of medieval date. Since the pottery was on the surface of the floor the dating of this structure is far from certain, but if it is medieval then it could be a shepherd or stockman's hut. An oval timber structure of similar size, but with a sunken floor, which was found inside an Iron Age enclosure at Fisherwick near Lichfield, was dated to the medieval period by the small quantity of pottery associated with it.

54 Probable house platform on Hodge Hill Common

MOATED SITES

Some of Birmingham's medieval dwellings were surrounded by moats. Moated sites consist of one or more ditches, which in most cases were intended to be water-filled, surrounding an area occupied by buildings or other structures. The earth created by digging the moat was often piled into the area enclosed by it to form a raised platform on which buildings were constructed. The size and shape of the area enclosed by the moat varies. Rectangular or near-rectangular enclosures are common but some are circular. Sometimes there is more than one enclosure, and the moat is often accompanied by one or more fishponds. Most moated sites were constructed between the twelfth and fourteenth centuries. Birmingham's moats are part of a concentration of moats in this part of the West Midlands, which extends into adjoining parts of Solihull, Warwickshire and Staffordshire. They are the medieval equivalent of Iron Age ditched farmstead enclosures like that at Langley Mill Farm described in Chapter 2. There were originally as many as ninety moated sites in what is now the city of Birmingham, almost all of them in the south and east of the city, but few of these are now visible because the buildings have long since disappeared and the moats themselves have been filled in and covered by modern development.

Although they would have kept out unwanted visitors, moats were not primarily defensive and were rarely accompanied by anything more than a low bank or fence. Although a wet moat could have other practical purposes or uses such as a source of water if fire broke out in the timber buildings it surrounded, the main reason for constructing a moat around a house is likely to have been prestige: the moat was one of a number of status symbols in the medieval period together with churches, monasteries, deer parks and castles. The moat made the building it surrounded stand out and look something like a castle even though it had no stone walls, towers or battlements.

Moats may surround isolated farmsteads or houses in villages and hamlets. Some of them surround manor houses. Many moated farmsteads are in areas where new land was being brought into cultivation by assarting (literally grubbing up trees and trees and bushes, but also a legal term) in the twelfth and thirteenth centuries. The moated farmstead would be surrounded by the enclosed fields resulting from this process, and the moat represented the status or assumed status of its owner.

Birmingham's moated sites reflect the variety of size, form, types of buildings enclosed, and status of owners observed elsewhere in the country. Excavations of varying extent have taken place at six of Birmingham's moated sites: Hawkesley Farm, Kents Moat, Gannow Green, Sheldon Hall, Weoley Castle and Birmingham manor house (also known as Birmingham Moat). The results of the excavations at Birmingham Moat have been described above. The excavated sites are all at the higher end of the social scale but nonetheless allow us to draw comparisons between the layout and types of buildings on these sites. Earthworks have been recorded at Peddimore Hall and Walmley Ash and many sites are known only from their depiction on historic maps.

Hawkesley Farm Moat

Adrian Oswald and Brian Roberts undertook excavations and observations at Hawkesley Farm in 1957-58 preceding and during the construction of bungalows and a tower block. Unlike some other moated sites, the earth dug out to construct the moat had not been used to form a platform on which the buildings were constructed but had been dumped to the north of the moat, outside the area enclosed by it. The entrance to the site was over a gap in the moat *(55)*. Post holes alongside the entrance gap, roof tile and hints of trenches for horizontal timber beams nearby might indicate a gatehouse. At the west corner there were traces of a sandy bank around the inner edge of the moat, possibly the eroded remains of a sandstone wall, and further north-east there were post holes which may indicate a fence. The earliest features were ditches, dated to the thirteenth century from pottery in them, which may have been dug to drain the site before any buildings were constructed. The ditches were overlain in the west corner of the site by beam slots (narrow trenches for horizontal beams which formed the base of timber-framed walls). These dated to the early fourteenth century and were interpreted as the walls of a long house, possibly with subdivisions. A pitched stone surface paving overlay the ditches and abutted these trenches *(56)*.

In the late fifteenth or early sixteenth century the stone surface and the beam slots were cut through by a hearth surrounded by a wooden screen or hut. At the other end of the beam slots there was a coal-fired oven with another beam slot around it. Rubble and coal from the oven including glazed roof tiles and fifteenth-century pottery overlay the beam slots. Stake holes indicated a screen, possibly a wind shield, around the oven's furnace. It had succeeded an earlier oven on the same site. To the north-east there was a line of large post holes with a large quantity of roof tile, some of it decorated and glazed. There were further post holes to the south east, whose stone packing (after removal of the posts) contained late sixteenth- or seventeenth-century pottery, and nearby there was another coal-fired oven. This and the other oven could have been used for a variety of purposes including cooking or malting grain for brewing, but at the time the excavation took place excavated deposits were not routinely sampled for laboratory analysis to detect seeds and other remains that could have provided such information. To the north-east of this, and adjoining the later farmhouse, there was a sandstone base, which was possibly a hearth, and a line of large post holes, which may have held one arcade of an aisled building.

Sandstone used in a later farmhouse on the site may have been reused from earlier timber buildings that rested on low stone walls, and indeed all the excavated medieval features may have been ancillary structures to a main

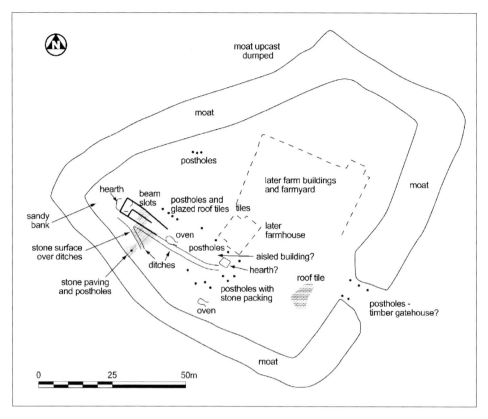

55 Excavated features at Hawkesley Farm Moat. *Compiled from plans by Adrian Oswald*

56 Hawkesley Farm Moat: excavations in the west corner of the site, looking west, showing ditch, stone surfaces and beam slots. *Copyright Birmingham Museums and Art Gallery*

building that lay on the part of the site occupied by the later farmhouse. Some of the undated features found in the excavation could be post-medieval in date.

Kent's Moat

Small-scale excavations at Kent's Moat in 1959 by Victor Skipp were followed by more extensive excavations by Ann Dornier in 1964 in advance of housing development. The moat, 9m (30ft) wide and 3.3m (11ft) deep, surrounded a roughly rectangular area about 78m by 54m (260 by 180 ft) *(57)*. A trench through the moat revealed that it had been cut through the natural red clay, and therefore would have held water without a lining. The water must have come from groundwater or a spring because there is no stream nearby. It had an earth bank on its inner edge with a rear revetment consisting of a single course of sandstone blocks. The front revetment was probably timber. Skipp excavated small areas on the moat platform and Dornier included much of the eastern half of the area enclosed by the moat, but the depth of her excavation was limited by the requirements of the new development and therefore the earliest periods of occupation may not have been reached *(58)*. The buildings on the site were all timber, resting on clay, clay and sandstone chips, or on unmortared sandstone blocks. The earliest period identified in the excavation, probably thirteenth century, included cobbling sloping down towards the edge of the moat near the north-east corner of the platform. The moat was presumably crossed by a bridge. There were also clay and clay and sandstone chip wall foundations towards the eastern side of the platform, and a rectangular timber building on the site later occupied by the hall may have been constructed in this period. Subsequently, in the early to mid-fourteenth century, a new entrance was established on the north of the site, where a cobbled area ran between two structures to the hall, a rectangular building with a central stone hearth and a clay floor in part of it. A building to the south at right angles to the hall may have been a solar. A structure to the east, interpreted as the kitchen, contained a tile-built hearth, and there was a coal storage area to its east. Another structure to its south had a stone hearth and clay floor and a spread of coal and to the north there was a stone-built structure with a clay floor containing a circular area, which was possibly the site of an oven. Ridged roof tiles were used as a drain near this.

In the middle of the fourteenth century the buildings at Kent's Moat were modified, largely through rebuilding on the same lines. The entrance was re-cobbled and large blocks were placed possibly as an abutment for a timber bridge over the moat. The hall was reduced in size, or realigned so that it lay north-south rather than east-west. The south wing was rebuilt, one of its walls using broken roof tiles. An area of rubble outside it may have been the base of a stair to a first floor. It was floored with decorated tiles, and fragments of coloured glass windows were found, possibly but not necessarily indicating

57 The south corner of Kent's Moat, showing the now-dry moat ditch

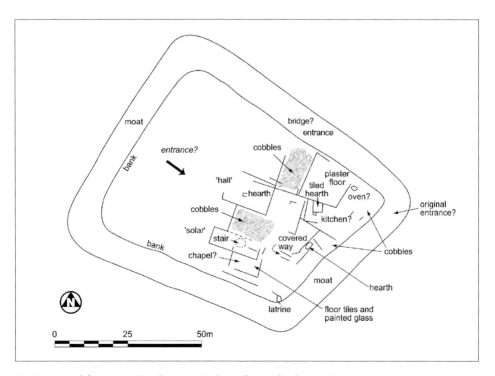

58 Excavated features at Kent's Moat. *Redrawn from a plan by Ann Dornier*

a chapel. A floor of decorated tiles was also laid in the north-east corner of the site and there was a plaster floor next to it. In the kitchen block, the tiled hearth was replaced by a larger one, and coal continued to be stored in the adjoining structure. A finely cobbled courtyard occupied the area between the kitchen and the solar and a complete cooking pot had been set into the cobbles. A covered way joined the kitchen to the solar block and there was a latrine built of mortared stone at the south-east corner, draining into the moat. Trenches in the western part of the moated area revealed no structures. There was no evidence for occupation of the site after the fifteenth century.

The incompleteness of the excavation in terms of area and depth, the complexity of structures and the potential invisibility of timber buildings once their stone footings are removed make it difficult to reassess the site. There may have been a more radical rearrangement of the site's layout between different phases than Dornier allows for.

The layout of buildings she interprets from the excavated evidence is unusual. We would expect the main entrance to the hall to be via a passage at one end of it, but there is no indication of this in the excavated remains. If the hall was aligned north-south in its later phase, then the entrance to the site might have been on the west, as in the later phase at Weoley Castle. The area in front of it might have deliberately been kept clear of structures to enhance the setting of the hall, and ancillary buildings kept to the rear or east of it.

If we accept Dornier's interpretation of the main buildings at Kent's Moat as a hall with linked or detached but adjoining buildings on two sides, it would then be similar to, although less regular than, the early buildings at Sheldon Hall as interpreted by Martin Cook from the existing structures, which consisted of freestanding or abutting wings at each end of a central range. During renovations he observed post holes, gullies and a pebble surface in trenches inside the existing central range, indicating a building predating it. The pattern of post holes suggested unevenly spaced bays on the alignment of the existing buildings. Further buildings beyond this were indicated by buried foundations observed in 1880 when they were picked out by frost in the surrounding grass. Excavations by Rowan Ferguson found medieval pottery ranging in date from the twelfth to the fifteenth centuries from within the moated area north of the existing building. She also found that the moat had been revetted on its inner side with a wall of bricks similar to those used in the central range of the building itself, the roof timbers of which have been dated by dendrochronology to 1617-19, as described below. Although she suggested that the brick moat wall was contemporary with the original construction of the moat, it is far more likely that the wall relates to tidying of the moat when the house itself was rebuilt and that the moat is actually medieval, particularly when there is other evidence for medieval occupation of the site. Excavations and observations also located part of the infilled moat on the east and south.

Gannow Green

At Gannow Green in Frankley, the moat surrounds a roughly rectangular area 60 yards long and 30 yards wide. Small-scale excavation by Brian Roberts in the 1960s showed that earth dug out to construct the moat had been piled up on top of the former ground surface to form a building platform 1.8m (6 ft) high. Under this the former turf line contained pollen of alder, hazel and oak from the woodland on the site when the moat was constructed, but there was also cereal pollen and a few grains of weeds of cultivation indicating some arable land in the vicinity. The moat was fed by a stream which flowed into the nearby River Rea. The west side of the moat was constructed along the original steam course, and an overflow channel for the stream was constructed parallel to the moat. The moat had been lined with clay to prevent water seeping out into the porous subsoil. Inevitably the clay lining needed to be renewed, and the moat filled with debris which needed cleaning out. The pottery from the site suggested that the moat was in existence in the thirteenth century and was recut in about 1270. There was a well-laid sandstone wall, constructed of dressed blocks, along the south edge of the moat platform, still surviving to a height of 1.3m (4ft) *(59)*. Excavation showed that it did not continue around all sides of the moat. Parts of it could also have served as the plinth for several timber buildings. The wall was related to a cleaning and relining of the moat and was suggested to be part of an unfinished rebuilding project during the fourteenth century. The moat puddling contained a scatter of roof tiles, including flat and curved ridge tiles, several of them crested, probably from a building constructed against the site's perimeter wall. On

59 The stone wall at Gannow Green Moat. *Copyright Birmingham Museums and Art Gallery*

60 Right The tiled hearth at Gannow Green Moat. *Copyright Birmingham Museums and Art Gallery*

61 Below Plan of Weoley Castle in the twelfth and early thirteenth centuries. *Compiled from plans by Adrian Oswald*

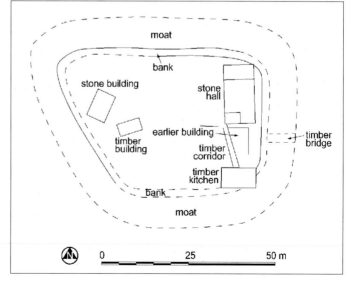

moat

bank

stone building

stone hall

earlier building

timber building

timber corridor

timber bridge

timber kitchen

bank

moat

0   25   50 m

the platform surface near the stone wall there was a layer of tile and quartzite cobbles, an insubstantial stone wall interpreted as a sill wall for a timber building, and a trench for a horizontal beam. Towards the north-east corner of the site there was a fifteenth-century hearth constructed of roof tiles set on edge and surrounded by sandstone blocks *(60)*, together with a stretch of robbed-out wall, a spread of sandstone and a pit.

Handsworth, Acocks Green and Longbridge

Anna Deeks's trenches in 2003 in what is now Maxwell Avenue in Handsworth where a moat is marked on an eighteenth-century map did not locate the moat itself, but a soil layer contained a few pieces of medieval pottery and a later feature was constructed of dressed sandstone blocks. At Colmers Farm Moat in Longbridge, sandstone blocks and cobbles exposed in a modern house garden were undated. Trenches at a moated site in Acocks Green revealed a pebble surface, a pit and part of the moat.

Weoley Castle

Excavations at Weoley Castle by Adrian Oswald showed that in its earliest periods it looked little different from other moated sites and consisted of a moat with a bank and a timber palisade surrounding two stone buildings and at least two timber buildings *(61)*. A comparison was made above between these periods at Weoley and the likely form of Birmingham's manor house. From the later thirteenth century onwards, though, rebuilding by the powerful de Somery family transformed Weoley Castle into a fortified manor house, in which the buildings were surrounded by a stone wall with towers as well as a moat.

The moat was fed with water from a stream. Its sides had to be puddled with clay to retain water because it was dug into porous sand and sandstone, and as at Gannow Green the puddling layers had to be renewed on several occasions. In its earliest period there was probably a palisade along the inner edge of the moat, supported to its rear by bracing posts whose angled sockets were found in the excavation. The moat was subsequently cleaned out and a gravel bank, with timber along its inner edge, replaced the palisade.

The earliest features in the area surrounded by the moat were contemporary with the palisade or the gravel bank. The very earliest structure on the site was an undated hearth or oven, which was found under the timber kitchen. There were also cobble and sandstone surfaces below the timber kitchen. The earliest building found in the excavations lay on the eastern side of the moated area between the early stone hall and the timber kitchen (both described below). Its walls were represented by post holes and beam trenches which indicated two phases of construction. It had a cobble floor, with an exterior cobbled path and stake holes beyond that. A substantial timber bridge provided access over the moat to this building, possibly to and from the fishpond if that existed at this period. The site as a whole may have been entered from the west, as in its later periods. Sandstone blocks used in the stone hall were reused and might have supported the timber walls of an earlier building. The date of the hearth, surfaces or buildings might be indicated by twelfth-century spouted pitchers made in Stamford, which were found in the moat.

These structures were replaced in the first half of the thirteenth century by a stone building, interpreted as a hall, which was connected by a covered timber corridor to a timber building, interpreted as a kitchen. This arrangement reduced the fire risk to the hall and ensured that hot food could be brought to it from the kitchen out of the weather. Both the hall and the kitchen postdated the gravel bank. They were accompanied by a timber building in the west part of the site and another stone building. The existence of a chapel at the north-west corner of the site was deduced from stone gargoyles found in the moat here.

The stone building interpreted as the hall was constructed of stone blocks reused from an earlier building. It probably had a thatch or shingle roof, since there is no evidence for tiles, and a plaster floor replaced by a timber floor. The latter contained a coin minted in 1248, which was in a good condition and had probably therefore been lost shortly after this. This building burned down. Outside it, there was a floor of cobbles set on clay, into which was set a slot for a wall of a timber corridor connecting it to the timber building. Below this there was cobbling forming a path between the two buildings, which predated the corridor. A fenced yard between the stone and timber buildings is interpreted as a farmyard. Organic layers in it containing stable flies are probably stable litter. There was a stone tower in the north-east corner of the moated area.

The timber building interpreted as the kitchen also dates to the first half of the thirteenth century. The dump of clay and sand over it, described below, had ensured moist conditions and excluded oxygen, preserving its timbers (62). The roof was supported by large upright posts at the corners of the building, which had intermediate uprights between them on the north wall, with sleeper beams between them. Additional vertical timbers were set into the horizontal sill beams to form a framework for the walls. The uprights were grooved to take horizontal weather-boarding. Thatch-like material on the floor of the building was probably from its roof. It had a cobbled floor. The building was divided into two rooms and was entered via the larger western one. The eastern room had a hearth, constructed of clay, sandstone and cobbles which was separated from the main wall by a sill beam with horizontal weather-boarding. Later, the western chamber was narrowed. In a second phase, one gable wall of the building was replaced with walls of vertical weather-boarding on a sleeper beam. The interior partitions were removed and it was converted into an aisled hall. The floor levels were raised twice.

Remains of these buildings and other structures surrounded by the first moat were covered and preserved under 1 to 1.3m (3 to 4ft) of material dumped

62 North wall of
the timber kitchen
at Weoley Castle.
Levels of succes-
sive floors are
indicated by the
skewers. *Copyright
Birmingham
Museums and Art
Gallery*

over them when a later larger moat was constructed enclosing a greater area.
Spoil from the enlargement of the moat and possibly from the construction of
the fishpond to its east was used to raise the area inside the moat, which was
now crossed by a drawbridge near its north-western corner. Oswald suggested
this enlargement and transformation followed the granting of a 'licence to
crenellate' (the King's permission to enclose a house with mortared stone
walls with towers and battlements) in 1264, when Weoley Castle became a
fortified manor house with a stone curtain wall with stone towers along it,
running alongside the inner edge of the enlarged moat *(63)*. The wall enclosed
a great hall, in the same location as the earlier stone building, with a stone
hearth; a kitchen, on the same location as the earlier timber building, with a
tile hearth to its east; a stone barn with a tiled roof; a building with a decorated
tile floor and painted glass windows which was probably a chapel; and stone
bases for timber buildings. Internal square stone bases were probably supports
for timber aisle posts, as in the building in the south-west of the walled area,
which when rebuilt in the fourteenth century had tiled roofs and a plaster
floor. Roof tiles from the site include ridge tiles decorated with crests, and
finials. An iron window grill and a timber door were found in the moat. A
survey of 1424 describes the buildings on the site at that time, which can
be identified to a large extent with the remains visible today. These include
a stable, bakehouse, brewhouse, chapel and guest rooms. The survey also

63 Wall, tower and moat at Weoley Castle

mentions an outer court containing a large barn. David Symons has identified the likely location and extent of this from field boundaries which are shown to the west of the site on the Northfield Tithe Map of 1840.

The objects found at Weoley Castle, particularly in its later periods, provide a vivid picture of aristocratic life in medieval Birmingham. In addition to pottery made in the Bull Ring and Deritend areas of Birmingham *(64)* and iron implements that may have been manufactured locally, objects from other parts of the country and continental Europe emphasise the site's status. Even the more mundane everyday items supplement the sparser finds from other medieval sites in Birmingham, such as the fragments of wooden bowls that were preserved in the same conditions as the timbers of the kitchen and must have been commonplace. Some of the iron tools, which included a pick, a turf cutter, chisels, gouges, and a stone-mason's hammer and punch *(65)* must be related to construction work rather than to something that was going on all the time, but axes, a bill hook, shears and a blacksmith's tongs were tools of everyday life. The smith's work included the door hinges found on the site as well as horseshoes. Horse bits and spurs were also found *(66)*. The bits may have been made by the predecessors of the Birmingham lorimers mentioned by John Leland in the sixteenth century. As well as providing everyday transport for the owners of Weoley Castle, the horses would have been used in hunting in the adjoining park, accompanied by the hunting dog whose skull was found. Arrows with the barbed iron heads found on the site

64 Pitcher and Deritend Ware jugs from Weoley Castle. *Copyright Birmingham Museums and Art Gallery*

65 An axe, chisels, gouge, and hammer and punch from Weoley Castle. *Copyright Birmingham Museums and Art Gallery*

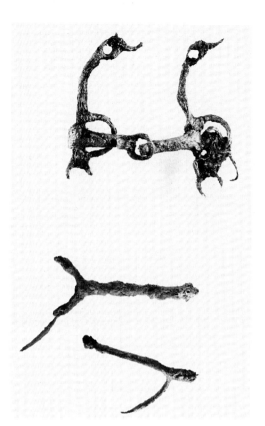

66 Left A horse bit and spurs from Weoley Castle. *Copyright Birmingham Museums and Art Gallery*

67 Below A barbed hunting arrow-head and other objects including a handle from Weoley Castle. *Copyright Birmingham Museums and Art Gallery*

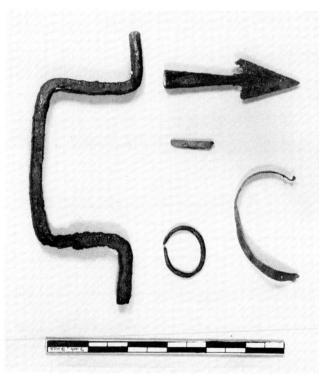

were shot at deer *(67)*. An archer with such an arrow is depicted on a floor tile from the site *(68)* and deer bones show that venison was eaten. An iron meat hook could have hung over the great hearth in the kitchen. Ladies spun using spindle whorls, men and women played the games indicated by a knight from a chess set made of antler and a jet die, and music was provided by the trumpet or bagpipes whose wooden mouthpiece was found. A fifteenth-century alembic or pottery retort containing mercury, probably the product of Spanish cinnabar suggests that alchemy, another pursuit of the rich, was being practised on the site *(69)*.

The range of imported items found at Weoley Castle had not been matched in Birmingham since the Roman period. It includes a fourteenth-century communion cruet of almost pure tin which may be English but could have been made in Spain *(70)*, copper-alloy lidded tankards possibly manufactured in Normandy, a range of pottery including French wares and fifteenth-century majolica from Valencia in Spain, and Syrian and Byzantine glass *(71)*. Moated sites were compared above to Iron Age farms in ditched enclosures. In its structures and in the range of objects used there, Weoley Castle in its later stages was more comparable to a Roman villa than to an Iron Age farm.

68 Floor tile from Weoley Castle show-ing an archer. *Copyright Birmingham Museums and Art Gallery*

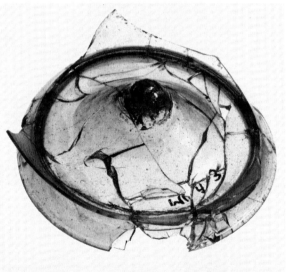

BUILDINGS IN MEDIEVAL BIRMINGHAM: MATERIALS AND APPEARANCE

The oldest surviving buildings in Birmingham other than churches are fifteenth century in date, but the excavated structures from the moated sites and from King's Norton date from the thirteenth to fifteenth centuries, with the exception of the possible twelfth-century structures at Birmingham Moat and Weoley Castle. No remains of houses have yet been found in the town centre but building materials have been found in thirteenth-century and later contexts.

Timber was the principal building material. The only wholly or mainly stone-built structures other than churches were the thirteenth-century building at Birmingham Moat, the thirteenth-century great hall and chapel at Weoley and their later replacements, and possibly buildings at Sutton Coldfield manor house. Dressed and mortared stone was used for the later surrounding wall and towers at Weoley Castle, and for perimeter walls at Gannow Green and possibly Hawkesley Farm. In each case the stone was obtainable near the site, but its extensive use, particularly for prominent features such as perimeter walls, suggests that it served as a status symbol as well as a durable building material. A fourteenth-century latrine at Kent's Moat was built of mortared stone. Stone was also used to line wells in the town centre and for hearths at Kent's Moat and Weoley Castle.

In timber buildings, horizontal beams rested on low stone walls at Primrose Hill Farm, Gannow Green and Kent's Moat and probably in the early buildings at Weoley Castle, and at Maxwell Avenue and possibly at Colmers Farm. The reused sandstone blocks at Wiggins Hill Farm, Hermitage Farm and Hawkesley Farm suggest that the medieval buildings on these sites were constructed like this. At Weoley Castle vertical posts were supported by stone bases. Horizontal beams set in trenches were used as the base for timber-framed walls at Hawkesley Farm and King's Norton. In the later phase at King's Norton and at Kent's Moat such beams rested on clay bases and were accompanied by posts on clay pads. Earth-fast posts were used in buildings at Hawkesley Farm and possibly at Sheldon Hall. Ground-based structures are probably under-represented because their recognition depends on conditions of survival and of excavation.

It is difficult to reconstruct building superstructures from the excavated remains, but a rectangular hall with one or two cross-wings was probably a standard layout in the moated houses and other high status sites. A hall

Opposite, clockwise from top left
69 Alembic from Weoley Castle. *Copyright Birmingham Museums and Art Gallery*

70 Communion cruet from Weoley Castle. *Copyright Birmingham Museums and Art Gallery*

71 Syrian painted and gilded glass from Weoley Castle. *Copyright Birmingham Museums and Art Gallery*

and cross-wing is also indicated in the excavated structure at King's Norton but here at least some cooking may have been done outside, in an oven like those found at Edgbaston Street in the city centre and Coleshill Street in Sutton Coldfield. The kitchens at Weoley Castle and probably at Kent's Moat were detached from the main building – a sensible fire precaution. The roofs of the stone halls at Weoley Castle and Birmingham Moat may have been supported by raised crucks (large curving timbers running from the wall to the apex of the roof) like that at Stokesay Castle in Shropshire, but the later thirteenth- and fourteenth-century timber halls probably had base crucks (curving timbers running from the base of the walls and supporting the roof timbers) like that in the great hall at West Bromwich Manor House, which has been dated by dendrochronology to 1275. Aisles seem only to have been used in ancillary structures such as barns, stables and possibly the timber kitchen at Weoley Castle. Dendrochronology shows that full crucks (curving timbers running from the base of the wall to the apex of the roof) were constructed in Birmingham in the first half of the fifteenth century. Their construction probably overlaps with that of buildings like Primrose Hill Farm.

Although the well-preserved remains of the timber kitchen at Weoley Castle show how walls may have been built at other sites in Birmingham, the use of weatherboarding seems an extravagant use of timber, and may reflect the special social status of this site even in its early phases or could be imitating an architectural tradition from elsewhere in the country. Wattle and daub would have sufficed here, and would have been the main wall infill material elsewhere. As well as being used for daub, clay was used for floors at Kent's Moat. Plaster floors were found at Kent's Moat and Weoley Castle and at both these sites some buildings had floors of decorated tiles. Floor tiles were also found at Birmingham manor house. Discoveries of floor tiles in Park Street and Floodgate Street are surprising for we would expect only churches and high status houses to have had such expensive floor coverings.

Roof tiles were used set on edge in a thirteenth-century oven at Edgbaston Street. Roof tiles, including glazed and crested ridge tiles, occur at Weoley Castle in the late thirteenth or early fourteenth century, Kent's Moat in the fourteenth century, Gannow Green in the fourteenth and fifteenth centuries, at Hawkesley Farm in the fifteenth century or earlier and at Moor Street, Edgbaston Street and Birmingham manor house. Roof tiles were also used in kitchen hearths at Weoley Castle, Kent's Moat and Gannow Green, and to make drains at Kent's Moat. The roofs of the thirteenth-century buildings at Weoley Castle and elsewhere could have been thatch or timber shingles. Heather, indicated by botanical remains on the city centre sites could have been used as a roofing material. No roof tiles were found at King's Norton showing that the fourteenth-century buildings here still had thatch or other roofs. The use of clay roof tiles in the city centre may have been intended to reduce the fire risk posed by fire-using industries and particularly prompted by the 'Great Fire of Birmingham' which took place at some time between 1281 and 1313. At the rural moated sites tiled roofs may have initially been a status symbol, but the greater use of tiles in the town centre could have resulted in increased production and made them more widely and cheaply available.

All of the material used in Birmingham's medieval buildings has implications for the availability and management of resources. Other than in churches, relatively small quantities of stone were used, and in all cases it was local sandstone. Timber and wood formed the bulk of building materials, with posts and planks coming from standard trees, possibly pollarded, and wattles of hazel, willow and alder from coppiced woodland, and osier beds. Heather was probably widely used as a roofing material as well as for animal bedding and would have been gathered from heathland such as Birmingham Heath, to the west of the town centre. Straw from local cereals could have been used for thatch and mixed with daub in walls. Clay, used unfired for daub walling and puddling the sides of moats and fired as roof and floor tiles, is widely available in Birmingham. Although no direct evidence has yet been found, the roof tiles used on buildings and to construct hearths from the thirteenth century onwards were almost certainly made locally. Decorated floor tiles at Weoley Castle and other sites were probably made near to the sites by itinerant tile makers. Pebbles and cobbles were locally obtained, as was sand for use in mortar, but lime for mortar and for the plaster floors at Weoley Castle and Kent's Moat must have been made from limestone from the Black Country to the north-west of Birmingham.

FISHPONDS AND WATERMILLS

The construction of moats to surround dwellings was just one part of medieval water engineering. Some Birmingham moated sites have adjoining or attached fishponds, providing an obligatory part of the medieval diet. The extent and location of the ponds at Gannow Green and other moated sites suggests that they may have been constructed for display as much as for fish and that they were another status symbol.

The pond at Weoley Castle has been mentioned above. Gannow Green moat is one of a series of features extending for about half a mile along the Rea valley. There were two fishponds to the east and one to the west of the moat, whose water was held back by dams; those to the east are now covered by modern housing but the dam of the pond to the west survives *(72)*. Mick Aston's plan of this in 1969 before the houses were built suggests that it included the original course of the River Rea, which was diverted into a new channel to the south *(73)*.

72 Fishpond dam at Mull Close, west of Gannow Green Moat

In some cases ponds were constructed by digging out hollows, as at Weoley, Peddimore and Langley; at others a stream was dammed, as at Gannow Green, and at Perry an existing hollow or pool was used. At Peddimore Hall a rectangular fishpond to the west of and upstream from the moat has channels running from it around the outside of the moat, which create a double moat. At Langley Hall there are two fishponds to the west of the moat *(74)*, and at Perry Hall a long pond to the south of the moat was probably a former course of the nearby River Tame. The deer park at Sutton Park contains three medieval fishponds, all constructed by damming streams with material derived from a quarry at the end of the dam. The detail of construction is unknown but since the quarried material here would have been mainly sand and gravel there must have at least been

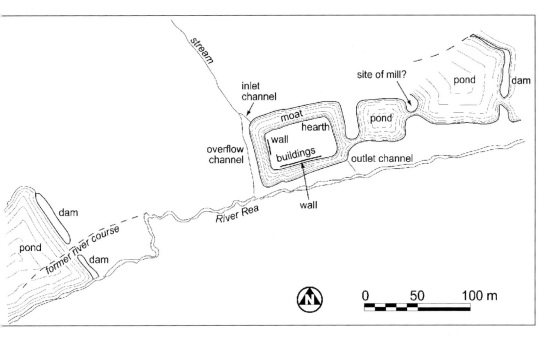

73 Gannow Green Moat and its fishponds. *Incorporating information on a plan by Mick Aston*

74 Two fishponds at Langley Hall

a turf capping to this to prevent percolation and erosion, and probably also puddling with clay brought in from elsewhere, as at the moats at Gannow Green and Weoley.

Some other, undated artificial ponds in Birmingham, some of them surviving only as dams, could be medieval. Several of Birmingham's many watermills are known to have existed in the Middle Ages but there are no surviving or excavated remains of mill buildings of this period. One of the ponds at Gannow Green could have powered a watermill: this may have been on the broad dam separating the two eastern pools. Gullies predating ridge and furrow at Walkers Heath may have channelled water from a stream for an industrial purpose, possibly textile processing.

USING THE LAND: FIELDS, CROPS, LIVESTOCK AND WOODS

The archaeological evidence for agriculture and other rural land use consists of structures such as estate boundaries, field and paddock boundaries, ridge and furrow, marl pits and wood boundaries, together with seeds and pollen of the crops that were being grown and bones and products of the animals that were being kept.

As noted in chapter 2, the field system around Lilycroft Farm respects Roman features and could itself be Roman in date, and the rectilinear field system at the Burrells may be Roman or earlier in origin. Other boundaries were however newly created in the medieval period. At Quinton Meadows a bank and ditch marks the boundary of the landholding of Howley Grange, which was an agricultural estate belonging to Halesowen Abbey by the thirteenth century. The hedge on this boundary contains five woody species which suggests that it is at least 500 years old. Other field boundaries marked by banks and ditches run up to this but do not cross it, showing that they are later in date, and their hedges also contain five or more species. A bank and ditch to the east of the moated site at New Hall in Sutton Coldfield probably divided the estate around it from the open common land beyond. At Gibbet Hill, also in Sutton Coldfield, a bank and ditch now within woodland is in an area which was, until the nineteenth century, unenclosed common land used for grazing, and could represent an encroachment that created a field or paddock. Banks and ditches in Fox Covert may be medieval boundaries.

It has already been suggested that the ditched areas at Minworth Greaves were paddocks, and the farmyard waste from Weoley Castle shows that livestock were kept in moated sites. The evidence for grazing animals in the centre of medieval Birmingham has been discussed above. Although documentary references show that cattle were being brought into the town from other areas, at least some of the hides made into leather by its tanners must have been from cattle reared locally.

Cathy Mould's trenching of an extensive area south-east of the moated site at Peddimore Hall revealed some of the surrounding medieval agricultural landscape. Up to 50cm (1ft 8in) of alluvium covered earlier features in the lower lying part of the site, along a former stream course. The earliest medieval activity consisted of long narrow ditched enclosures bounded by gullies, some of which contained thirteenth- or fourteenth-century pottery. Some of the gullies were quite close to each other, suggesting recutting, or possibly related to stock management and forming droveways. The gullies found at Peddimore have the same dimensions as those prescribed in 1301-02 at Dunton when permission was given to improve the waste in accordance with the 'Assize of the Chase' – the ditches were to be no wider than 3ft 6in (1.05m) and the banks no higher than 1ft 6in (45cm). At Peddimore in the thirteenth century it was specified that does and their fawns must be able to leap over field boundaries.

Remains of ridge and furrow were also found in the Peddimore excavation, indicating former cultivation, and traces of it were visible on aerial photographs beyond the area excavated. Ridge and furrow also survives as earthworks just outside the moat at Peddimore Hall. To the south-west there are slightly curving ridges each 7 to 8m across, to the north-east ridges 3m wide overlie lower, broader ridges and to the north more ridge and furrow was recorded in 1972 but has since been levelled.

Ridge and furrow represents a cultivation method in which soil was ridged up to increase soil depth and improve drainage. Like field boundaries, ridge and furrow is difficult to date in isolation. Wider, higher curving ridges tend to be medieval and narrower, lower straight ridges post-medieval but narrower ridges also occur at earlier dates. In Birmingham, ridge and furrow at Walkers Heath, whose ridges are 4m to 7m wide, overlies gullies dated to the thirteenth to fourteenth century by pottery in them and therefore must be later in date than this.

Features overlying or cutting through it show the date by which ridge and furrow went out of use. At Minworth Greaves the Birmingham and Fazeley Canal of 1789 was constructed obliquely across ridge and furrow with ridges 5m to 7m wide and spoil from the canal's construction overlies it, and at Hawkesley ridge and furrow is overlain by the spoil mounds from the construction of the Wasthill Tunnel for the Worcester Canal at the beginning of the nineteenth century. Ridge and furrow is often associated with the open field system of medieval agriculture in which each ridge corresponded to a strip holding in the field. The ridges often have a reversed-S shape, resulting from the oxen team used to plough them having to begin to turn before the end of each furrow. At Minworth Greaves the ridges correspond to strips of land in an open field, which is shown on a map of 1791 and was still in use when the canal was constructed, but the ridge and furrow at Peddimore Hall, at Hawkesley near Hawkesley Hall and near

75 Medieval pottery found in fieldwalking in Sutton Coldfield

the moat at Perry Hall was never part of open fields and represents the use of this type of cultivation by the occupants of these moated sites.

Although some of them may have been brought in from beyond the area of the present city, we can be fairly confident that most of the crops whose seeds and pollen have been found in medieval deposits on Birmingham sites were grown locally. In the medieval town centre of Birmingham there were charred grains of wheat, barley, oats and rye, and seeds and pollen of hemp and flax, and the oven in Sutton Coldfield contained charred rye. Rye may have been a particularly significant crop in parts of the Birmingham area because it tolerates sandy soils. Also, its long straw is used for thatching.

Most of the medieval pottery found in fieldwalking in the Sutton Coldfield area had probably been thrown onto dung heaps and middens with other domestic refuse and subsequently spread on fields as fertiliser *(75)*. It therefore indicates the extent of cultivated land as well as the types of pottery in use. The absence of medieval pottery from land which was not cultivated and used as common grazing land in the eighteenth and early nineteenth centuries shows that this was its use in the medieval period as well. However, the probable house platform at Hodge Hill Common and the boundary at Gibbet Hill indicate encroachment onto common land.

Some of the many 'marl pits' in the parts of the city on Mercia Mudstone may have been dug in the medieval period to extract clay that was spread on fields to improve water retention in well-drained soil and to very slightly lime it. The pits are characteristically on upper parts of fields for ease of spreading the marl or alongside roads. Clay could have been dug from some of the pits for building, in daub for walls of for floors, hearths or ovens. Another use might have been for pottery production.

Coppiced woodland had to be securely enclosed with a stock-proof barrier to prevent grazing animals eating young coppice shoots. The boundary usually consisted of a bank and ditch, with the ditch on the outside and a hedge or fence on the bank. Like field boundaries, wood boundaries are difficult to date but substantial bank and ditch boundaries like that around Bromwich Wood in Bartley Green are likely to be medieval.

A bank and ditch forming the estate boundary at New Hall in Sutton Coldfield may have originated as a woodland boundary. Within the area investigated at Peddimore, and adjoining a former stream channel, there was an oval enclosed area which had tree boles inside, covered in charcoal, suggesting that it was a protected area of woodland in which the trees had eventually been felled and burned. However, the enclosure and woodland may be prehistoric in date because the tree bole and gully defining its eastern side were overlain by alluvium.

DEER PARKS

Deer parks – areas enclosed primarily to keep deer for hunting – are a special and exclusive use of land. The excavated deer park boundary ditch in the Bull Ring area of the city centre has already been described. Sutton Park was created as a deer park by 1126, within the hunting reserve of Sutton Chase. Post-medieval use of the site, particularly for animal grazing and recreation, and the absence of significant building or agricultural activity have ensured the survival as earthworks of not only much of the outer boundary but also internal subdivisions and fishponds.

Sutton Park lies to the west of the town of Sutton Coldfield, on sandy, pebbly soils which are unsuitable for cultivation because water percolation has washed nutrients out of them and they are prone to erosion and drying out. The creation of a deer park was a good economic use of such poor soils but the deer park was primarily created for recreation and to serve as a status symbol. The outer boundary of the medieval deer park consists of a ditch about 5m wide running inside the present park boundary (76), accompanied by a bank which is now followed by the park boundary fence but would originally have been topped by high oak paling. This would have formed the characteristic deer park boundary; a barrier too high and wide for deer to jump over. The ditch and bank are only visible on the north, west and part of the east side of the present park. On the south, land was taken out of the park in the sixteenth century, and on the north-east land was taken out in two successive pieces to create a park around Four Oaks Hall, first in 1756 and later in 1827, when land was added to the east of the park. The original shape of the deer park would have been nearly circular, ensuring that the maximum area was enclosed for the minimum perimeter. It includes two streams that were dammed to form fishponds, as described above.

The park is subdivided into separate enclosures, each of which is bounded by a bank and ditch, with the ditch on the inner side. On the east side of the park, a bank and ditch 5.5m wide in total forms a semi-oval enclosure centred on the manor house and including some of the fishponds and areas of woodland enclosed in the sixteenth century. A further bank and ditch about 7m wide appears to be an addition to the earlier subdivision and shares its western edge but diverges from it to the north and slightly to the south. A third subdivision forms a large irregularly-shaped enclosure, which shares part of the line of the other subdivisions and includes all but one of the woodland areas enclosed in the sixteenth century and the whole of the stream feeding Bracebridge Pool. Small excavations in 2001 across the lines of the latter two boundaries near Keepers Pool revealed no trace of any boundary feature on top of the banks (77). It is unlikely that any post holes for a fence or root channels for a hedge had been completely eroded away, so there may have been a dead hedge that would form a stockproof boundary but would only require anchoring by stakes rather than posts. The first two subdivisions might have been used to round deer into for ease of hunting, or to segregate different ages of deer, or might be earlier boundaries of the deer park. The third subdivision seems to have been constructed to protect woodland and water supply. It may have been matched by a similar enclosure on the west of the park, which is also bounded by a bank and ditch and may have included Longmoor Brook and Streetly Wood, but large parts of this boundary have been levelled in areas that were ploughed up in the Second World War and the full extent of the enclosure cannot now be traced.

FUELS

Coal was used as a fuel from the thirteenth century on sites in the city centre, as a fuel in the kitchen at Kent's Moat in the early to mid-fourteenth century and in the ovens at Hawkesley Farm in the fifteenth century. It must have been brought in from the Black Country or north Warwickshire. Coal was being used for smithing at Park Street, and at Hawkesley Farm it may have been specially selected in preference to wood to heat the ovens. At other city centre sites, possibly including the manor house it was used as a domestic fuel and at Kent's Moat it seems to have been used for cooking, suggesting a more

76 The ditch of the medieval deer park boundary at Sutton Park

77 Excavation of bank and ditch marking subdivision of Sutton Park

general and widespread use. However, on higher status sites like Kent's Moat, Hawkesley and Birmingham manor house the use of this expensive fuel might have been a status symbol like the moats themselves. The use of coal might also indicate a shortage of wood other than brushwood for fuel. The heavy use of timber and wood for construction and other purposes might have depleted the extensive woodland of the twelfth and thirteenth centuries that was indicated by pollen and seeds in the Bull Ring and by pollen at Gannow Green. Burnt peat was found in the Moor Street excavation, showing that this fuel was used, as it was in later periods, and it might have been the normal fuel of poorer people where it was available.

GETTING ABOUT

A wide range of goods including building materials, agricultural produce, industrial raw materials, finished products and fuels, was being carried into, out of, and around Birmingham in the medieval period. The archaeological evidence indicates or suggests what was being carried where.

Items brought into Birmingham included, at one extreme, the foreign items from overseas such as those found at Weoley Castle, but these were few, relatively small items. More significant were agricultural products, fuels, industrial raw materials, building materials and pottery, some of which were from Birmingham itself and others from further afield. Building timber and bark for tanning might have been brought in from outside Birmingham. Cattle, and possibly some crops, would have come from a greater distance as well as from the Birmingham area itself. Coal, iron, lime (for tanning and for mortar) and white clay used as a slip on Birmingham-made Deritend Ware pottery could all have come from the Black Country to the north-west. Pottery itself was also coming from Wednesbury in the Black Country and South Staffordshire as well as from Coventry, Worcester, and Buckinghamshire. At the same time leather, cloth, pottery vessels and metal items, the products of Birmingham's industries, were being taken out to surrounding areas.

In the absence of navigable rivers, roads were the only form of transport in Birmingham before the construction of canals. Many major and minor roads in the city follow routes in use in the medieval period and earlier. Some indication of the form of medieval roads is provided by hollow ways such as Bell Holloway and Yardley Green Road (78), which leads to a crossing of the River Cole. In some cases the hollow ways have been abandoned altogether and survive as earthworks, such as the former line of Bristol Road, replaced by a turnpike road on the present course, and in others they have been modified, such as Oxleys Road and Bulls Lane, which were narrowed in nineteenth-century land enclosures but whose former edges are still visible in adjoining fields.

78 Yardley Green Road hollow way

FROM MEDIEVAL TO MODERN

Medieval Birmingham is not distant and remote. It laid the foundations of the modern city in many ways. Much of the street pattern of the medieval town centre is still in use, and even the narrow rectangular 'burgage plot' land divisions are still property boundaries in Digbeth. Across the entire area of the modern city the major roads (before the advent of ring roads, by-passes and motorways) and many minor roads are routes used in the Middle Ages. The medieval villages have become the city's suburbs.

In addition to the market there was also a range of industries in the medieval town of Birmingham. It was dependent on its rural surroundings for foodstuffs and industrial raw materials. Coal, iron and other materials were being obtained from the Black Country. The development of Birmingham as a market and manufacturing town stimulated the growth of industries in the Black Country as well as agricultural production in its immediate vicinity.

By comparing the archaeological evidence from the town with that of rural settlements, we can see that a change in the form of the town in the fifteenth and sixteenth centuries, possibly related to greater industrialisation, correlates with new building in rural areas. The social status of settlements is also apparent from the types of pottery, fuels used and materials used in buildings. Locally made pottery was used at Minworth Greaves, pottery from more distant sources was found at King's Norton, and pottery imported from continental Europe reached the town centre and Weoley Castle. Houses in the town centre and on moated sites used coal for fuel and had tiled roofs, but those at King's Norton and Minworth Greaves did not. Parish churches and Weoley Castle were the only buildings in which stone was used in large quantities.

Beyond the town centre, moated sites were the first country houses, using architectural style, building materials and stretches of water as status symbols. Right at the top of the social scale, Weoley Castle is a medieval version of Aston Hall: had the de Somery family, Weoley's owners, been living in the seventeenth century, perhaps this is what they would have built.

CHAPTER 5
INTO THE MODERN CITY: THE LAST 500 YEARS

In contrast to earlier periods, there is a huge quantity of written records, maps and illustrations from the past few centuries telling us about people and places in Birmingham, and it might be thought that archaeology can add little or nothing to this. However, the archaeological evidence throws new light on this apparently familiar and well-documented recent past. Despite its quantity, the documentary evidence is inevitably fragmentary and variable in detail. It reflects not only the vagaries of survival but also a desire or requirement to make a record in the first place, and it can be coloured by the background and opinions of the person who made or was instructed to make that record. The archaeological evidence can also be fragmentary and difficult to interpret but it provides information on places, lifestyles and processes that are either not recorded in documents at all, or only partially. Below and above ground archaeological remains augment and sometimes contradict the documentary evidence *(79)*.

Much of the archaeological evidence for this period relates to industry, including workplaces, power sources, raw materials, products and waste products, sometimes reused, and the transport network that carried them, particularly canals. The archaeological evidence emphasises the sheer range of industries in Birmingham, including those not normally associated with the city, and the relationship between different industries. Excavations in the city centre have revealed remains of metalworking, leather tanning, bone working, hemp and flax processing, button making and brick, tile and pottery manufacture *(80)*. Excavations at the Soho Manufactory site in Handsworth and excavations and detailed recording at the former gasworks in Gas Street in the city centre have complemented the documentary evidence for these industrial sites.

However, the archaeological remains of sixteenth- to twentieth- century Birmingham are not solely those of industry. People living in the city centre and elsewhere were acquiring items from further afield than before. The

Hillwood Common
Hill Hook
Fox Hill
Sutton Park
Barn Farm
Langley Mill Farm
Holy Trinity Church
West Bromwich Manor House
St Bernard's Road
New Hall Mill
Fox Hollies
Peddimore Hall
Hamstead
Tower Hill
Plants Mill
Hill House
Jubilee Pit
Witton Hall
Minworth
Sandwell Priory/Hall
Witton
Oak House
Hilltop
Aston Hall
Hodge Hill Common
Soho
Saltley
Sheldon Hall
CITY CENTRE
(see separate map)
Blakesley Hall
Harrison's Road
Edgbaston Mill
California
Cannon Hill Park
Hay Hall
Airport
Woodgate Valley
Weoley Castle
Moseley
Highbury
Sarehole/ Trittiford
Canals
Wychall Mill
Northfield Mill
Kings Norton
Monyhull
Tunnel
0   5miles
0   4   8km

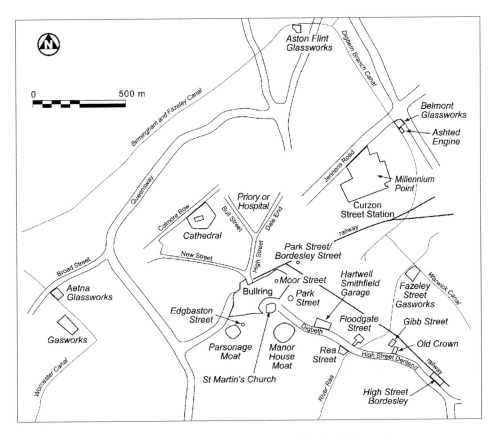

Aston Flint
Glassworks

Digbeth Branch Canal

Belmont
Glassworks

Ashted
Engine

0   500 m

Birmingham and Fazeley Canal

Jennens Road

Millennium
Point

Queensway

Priory or
Hospital

Curzon
Street Station

Colmore Row

Bull Street

Dale End

railway

Cathedral

New Street

High Street

Park Street/
Bordesley Street

Broad Street

Aetna
Glassworks

Moor Street

Hartwell
Smithfield
Garage

Warwick Canal

Fazeley
Street
Gasworks

Bullring

Park
Street

Edgbaston
Street

Floodgate
Street

Gibb Street

Old Crown

Gasworks

Digbeth

Parsonage
Moat

Manor
House
Moat

Rea
Street

High Street Deritend

railway

Worcester Canal

St Martin's Church

River Rea

High Street
Bordesley

79 *Opposite* Post medieval sites mentioned in the text. *Based on the Ordnance Survey map and reproduced by permission of Ordnance Survey on behalf of the Controller of Her Majesty's Stationery Office,* © *Crown Copyright 100042011*

80 *Above* Medieval and post medieval sites in the city centre mentioned in the text. *Based on the Ordnance Survey map and reproduced by permission of Ordnance Survey on behalf of the Controller of Her Majesty's Stationery Office,* © *Crown Copyright 100042011*

status and appearance of the city centre changed over time. Houses were built or rebuilt in the country, and some acquired ornamental gardens and parks. Woodland was managed, previously open land enclosed into fields, and sporting facilities constructed. Burial and memorial of the dead has also been investigated, together with remains of military training, munitions manufacture and wartime defences.

METALWORKING

John Leland's observation in his visit of about 1540 that 'a great parte of the towne is mayntayned by smithes' demonstrates the importance of metalworking in the Bull Ring, Digbeth and Deritend. The archaeological evidence indicates not only smithing but also casting.

At Floodgate Street near the River Rea, iron slag suggests metalworking in the sixteenth and early seventeenth centuries, and some of the features interpreted as part of a leather tannery, described below, could have originally been constructed for metalworking and later used to dump tanning waste, such as the large tank and the pipe feeding it, which was constructed in the middle of the sixteenth century. In the Bull Ring area the seventeenth and eighteenth centuries seem to have been a particularly busy period after an apparent lull in activity in the fifteenth and sixteenth centuries. At Park Street, for example, most of the evidence for metalworking is from the late sixteenth century to the middle of the eighteenth century. Iron smithing is represented by slag, smithing hearth bottoms which include fragments of coal, vitrified hearth lining, and hammer scale (fragments of iron resulting from hammering hot metal in a forge). Casting items in brass, other copper alloys and pewter, represented by copper alloy slag, and residues of copper, zinc and tin in crucibles, starts in the seventeenth century. Elsewhere in the city centre, walls and pebble surfaces which were possibly part of a smithy, a smithing hearth bottom, slag and hammer scale were found in High Street Bordesley and crucibles from the Birmingham Moat site had copper zinc residues. Excavations revealed extensive remains of the 19th century Cambridge Street Works, Birmingham's largest brassworks, alongside a canal basin.

Metalworking was not confined to the city centre. Water mills in the surrounding area forged and sharpened tools, and melted, rolled and drew metal. As well as the remains of the mills and their pools and leats, some of which are described below, rural metalworking has left its own debris, including crucible pots like those found at Park Street and other sites. These hard-fired pots were discarded once they became filled with residues but could then be used for other purposes. Crucible pots laid on their sides to serve as a field wall near Fox Hollies in Sutton Coldfield were originally used from the 1760s to make steel at Plants Mill for the wire works at Penns Mill. In south Birmingham, crucible pots have been used in walls at Highbury

81 Crucible wall near Harborne Golf Course

Hall, Harborne Golf Course *(81)* and War Lane in Harborne. The Harborne crucibles are from Harborne Mill, which made steel in the nineteenth century. At Wychall Mill, excavations showed that the tail race was lined with them. Excavations at Aston Hall, described below, showed that the main walls of the seventeenth-century house had been constructed on a foundation of iron furnace slag, which would have been brought from Aston Furnace, owned by the Holte family, builders and owners of Aston Hall.

ANIMAL AND VEGETABLE: BONE, HORN, LEATHER, CLOTH, ROPE AND BUTTONS

Bone and horn working were almost certainly practised in the medieval period, and continued into later centuries. Iron knives would have been one of the metal products made by the smiths at Park Street, and a cutler there may have been making both blades and handles. Wedge-shaped pieces of bone found in seventeenth-century deposits on the site are probably waste from the manufacture of knife handles. Some of the water-filled pits and tanks at this site might have been used to soak bone to soften it for working. At Floodgate Street near the River Rea a bone offcut suggests bone working, and the large quantity of sheep foot bones might have been brought to the site to make knife handles, for which they were well suited. Many of the bony cores of cattle horns found here had cut marks around the base resulting from removal of horn. This could similarly have been used for handles.

Birmingham's leather tanning industry continued into the post-medieval period. At Edgbaston Street tanning shifted from the western part of the site to the south-eastern side, further from the street frontage. Pottery shows that the earlier tanning pits on the western part of the site were filled in during the later sixteenth century but tanning continued. New tanning pits were dug, together with pits to contain lime, the caustic material used in the first stage of the tanning process. One of the pits was either timber lined or the barrel in which the lime had arrived on the site had been sunk into the ground. It was covered with a wooden lid to keep the lime dry. A barrel or cask was also used to store lime at Floodgate Street. Another pit contained the horn cores that were a waste product of the industry. Leather offcuts suggest leather working as well as tanning. Shallow rectangular pits were constructed on the other side of the site in the seventeenth century. These contained wood chips or sawdust and may have been for curing rather than tanning, or for the skins of smaller animals than cattle. There was a major change on the site in the early eighteenth century, when the pits were filled in.

The change in focus of the Edgbaston Street tannery, away from the part of the site nearest the street frontage, is reflected by the fact that tan yards newly established in this period are further away from the area around St Martin's church, down towards the River Rea. As the settlement grew, less land was available for an industry that required space for the various processes involved. By this time, too, although tanning was still an important Birmingham industry, metalworking had become prominent.

A sixteenth- to eighteenth-century tannery was excavated in Floodgate Street adjacent to the River Rea (82). A large tank or pool about 9m wide, 1m deep and at least 20m long had been constructed on what was then an island between two channels of the River Rea. It contained large quantities of wood, pottery, leather, animal hair and animal bone, including many horn cores. Leats on two opposite corners, each containing a covered timber drain, filled it and regulated the depth of water in it (83). Dendrochronology showed that one of the drains was made from a tree cut down between 1519 and 1550, and there was also late fifteenth- or early sixteenth-century pottery. As suggested above, this may relate to metalworking on the site before tanning took place. A pit containing cattle horn cores and pottery of middle to late seventeenth-century date was later dug into the backfilled tank. There were also pits containing lime, one of them lined with staves from a barrel or cask. Dendrochronology showed that the sequence of tree-ring widths in the staves was best matched by timber from western France. Unfortunately only heartwood survived so the barrel could not be precisely dated but the last ring was 1540 therefore the barrel must be later than this. There were also circular and rectangular pits. In the eighteenth century these structures were replaced

82 Excavations at Floodgate Street showing the central tank or pool. The small white circles are lime storage pits

83 Covered timber drain at Floodgate Street

with square brick structures, brick bases possibly for wooden vats, sunken brick vats and brick-lined wells. These structures are depicted on William Westley's drawing of Birmingham of 1732.

On the other side of the River Rea, at Gibb Street near the Custard Factory, there were five successive eighteenth-century timber-lined tanning pits and three wells. One of the tanning pits contained fragments of bark. Horn cores had been thrown into disused clay pits nearby.

As with metalworking, the leather industry was not confined to the city centre. For example, a mill pool was constructed at Blackroot in Sutton Park to drive a mill for leather-dressing.

Hemp seeds, pollen and stalks from Park Street, hemp pollen and seeds from the post-medieval fill of Birmingham Moat and hemp stalks from a seventeenth- or eighteenth-century pool or water channel near the River Rea in Rea Street are evidence for retting this plant by immersion in water to break down the fibres to make rope or sackcloth. The many watercourses in the area could have been used for this process. Flax seeds were also found at Park Street in this period and as earlier they could have reached the site as food or on plants brought for their fibres, to make linen. There was a flax mill at Moat or Malt Mill near the manor house in the eighteenth century. Two plank-lined tanks at Park Street may have been used in processing textiles, possibly dyeing. One of them may have had a wicker canopy over it.

Button manufacture was an important eighteenth- and nineteenth-century Birmingham industry. As well as metal, buttons were made from bone and shell. Pieces of bone from which circles have been cut by a stamping machine as blanks for buttons have been found at the Soho Manufactory. Similar waste pieces result from the manufacture of buttons from shell. In the watercourse on Edgbaston Street there were discs of mother-of-pearl that were button blanks and pieces of mother-of-pearl with the circular holes from which they had been cut. This was an extensive industry: pieces of shell with circular and semicircular cuts were also found at Gibb Street, and large pieces of unworked shell from Indian Ocean species at Floodgate Street must have been brought there for button manufacture. Remains of a nineteenth-century button manufactory were found on High Street Deritend, opposite the Old Crown.

MINERAL: POTTERY, PIPES, TILES, BRICKS AND LIME

Two of the few raw materials occurring in usable quantities within Birmingham, water and clay, come together in the manufacture of pottery, tiles and bricks. We have seen the evidence for a Roman pottery industry and for pottery manufacture in the city centre in the medieval period. In later centuries the little more than local market served by these was amply catered for by potters from other centres which had coal resources, obviously Stoke-on-Trent but also nearer to hand at Wednesbury and other places in the Black Country. Coarseware bowls and jars, Blackware cups and yellow ware cups and bowls probably made in Wednesbury from the sixteenth to eighteenth centuries have been found in excavation on several Birmingham sites and in fieldwalking in the Sutton Coldfield area. Birmingham was obtaining its coal from Wednesbury by the eighteenth century and probably for several centuries before that, and the pottery would have travelled along the same route as the coal. Waste pottery from Floodgate Street shows that flowerpots, with holes in their bases and the lower part of their walls, were manufactured on or near to this site in the seventeenth or early eighteenth centuries: they would have housed plants in the large gardens shown behind houses on maps such as William Westley's of 1731. Not surprisingly, pieces of similar pots were found at Park Street where such a house and garden would have stood in the eighteenth century. Part of a saggar, a vessel in which smaller pots were placed in a kiln to protect them from direct heat, was found in High Street Bordesley in an eighteenth-century deposit, suggesting pottery manufacture on this site as well. A large pit here, which was filled in during the seventeenth or eighteenth centuries, was probably dug to extract clay, as were pits at Gibb Street. In the nineteenth century pottery was made at Belmont Row and a short-lived enterprise produced craft pottery at Fox Hill in Sutton Coldfield. A brick-built bottle-shaped kiln of about 1830 has a central circular area inside it, which was where the pottery was fired, and the scar of another kiln attached to it *(84)*. An adjoining pond occupies a pit resulting from clay extraction. John Sutherland Valentine, who owned the site from about 1826 but had sold it by 1840, constructed 'furnaces' here for the manufacture of pottery.

Clay pipes were another fired clay product made in Birmingham. Fragments of the distinctive muffle, the lining that protected the pipes in the kiln, were found at the Birmingham Moat site and consisted of burnt clay with clay pipe stems embedded in it. Seventeenth-century clay pipe bowls were found on other parts of the site but it is not known whether or not they were made there. Unlike the pottery made at Floodgate Street and the tiles and bricks described below, clay pipes were made of white or yellowish clay, which would have had to be brought in from elsewhere, possibly from Wednesbury.

Bricks were used in the structure of the Roman pottery kiln in Sutton Coldfield and a few bricks have been found in medieval contexts in the city centre, but although the earliest brick buildings in Birmingham are early seventeenth- or possibly sixteenth century in date bricks did not replace timber as the principal building material until the later seventeenth or earlier eighteenth centuries.

The roof tiles used on buildings and to construct hearths in the Bull Ring and at Weoley Castle in the thirteenth century were almost certainly made locally, but no direct evidence for this industry has yet been found. Pits in Heath Mill Lane and High Street Bordesley were probably dug to extract clay

for brick or tile manufacture. They were being infilled in the seventeenth century, and were therefore disused by then.

There were three types of brick and tile production: for specific buildings, at all periods where they were not already being made nearby; small-scale industry, from the medieval period to the nineteenth century; and the large-scale industry of the nineteenth and early twentieth centuries that was fundamental to the city's development. Until well into the nineteenth century bricks and tiles for rural buildings in locations where suitable clay was readily available were made near those buildings. For example, in the field just to the east of the nineteenth-century Barn Farm some existing hollows and a large dark circle indicating a filled-in pit surround a blackened area with many fragments of brick and tile, some of them misshapen: the site of a brick and tile kiln. Clay for brick-making was dug out of the Mercia Mudstone (Keuper Marl) a short distance below the surface and when each pit became too deep to easily extract the clay another was dug. The 'kiln' need not have been much more than a bonfire built over the bricks and tiles that had been allowed to dry before firing. Pits and ponds next to brick farmhouses, where they are not remnants of medieval moats, may have been dug for clay for brick-making. Similarly some 'marl pits' may have originally been dug for brick-making.

Brick and tile manufacture at an industrial level took place in the Mercia Mudstone area in east Birmingham (Saltley, Yardley, Acocks Green), in the south-west at Bartley Green and in the north-west at Hamstead. Documentary evidence shows that roof tiles were being made in Yardley in the fifteenth century and the mid-nineteenth-century map accompanying the Tithe Award for this parish indicates many small tile and brick works. Brick manufacture at Saltley from the late nineteenth century onwards provided bricks for factories and for the rows of terraced houses in which their workers lived. Although nothing is now visible above ground, excavations revealed a late nineteenth century 'Scotch' open-topped brick kiln which was roughly rectangular, measuring 10m long and 5m wide. The clay pits were characteristically large with steep edges, as detected in excavation in Saltley where excavations showed that they were even more extensive than previously thought. Part of the claypits of the Hamstead Brickworks near Tame Valley Canal survive as an open space amidst housing. The brick industry of east Birmingham is now best seen in its products where the name of a particular brickworks has been stamped in the brick, such as the bricks from the Adderley Park works in Saltley used in a wall in Holliday Street in the city centre. Slaked lime made by heating limestone was used in building, various industrial processes and agriculture. Three brick built lime kilns of the 1820s excavated in Selly Oak burnt limestone brought from Dudley along the Dudley No. 2 Canal.

84 Opposite Pottery kiln at Fox Hill

85 Geophysical survey at Lower Tylers, Woodgate Valley. The hollow behind the surveyor is a clay pit

The large brick and tile industry in the California part of Bartley Green, which began in the middle of the nineteenth century close to the east portal of the Lapal Tunnel on the Dudley no.2 Canal, was not a new industry for this area. Archaeological and documentary evidence shows that there were smaller brick and tile making enterprises here at an earlier date. These may have been set up following construction of the canal, which brought coal for their fuel, towards the end of the eighteenth century. Clay could be dug on the kiln sites themselves. Field names on the Northfield Tithe Map of 1840 include several fields with names like 'Tile House' or 'Brick House' but there is no indication on the map of any kilns in these fields, so they must have gone out of use by this time. In some of these, and in other fields in the area, much of which is now Woodgate Valley Country Park, there are pits that were almost certainly dug to extract clay. One of the pits lies on the edge of a field called 'Lower Tylers' *(85)*. A geophysical survey by Ruth Murdie and her students around this pit revealed an area of burning about 30m across and two parallel lines which possibly represented the flues in the kiln. The flues were channels along which carried heat from a fire stoked outside the kiln. Bricks would be stacked over the flues. Excavations in Big Tile House revealed overfired waste bricks.

GLASSMAKING

Although glassmaking in the West Midlands in this period is normally associated with Stourbridge and Dudley, documentary research has identified 18 glassworks in Birmingham dating from the late eighteenth to the mid-nineteenth century. One of the earliest was in Edgbaston Street and its location is indicated by the name 'Glasshouse Court' on a map of 1808. Excavations here showed that debris from the glassworks had been thrown into the water channel that originally joined the two medieval moats on this site. All but the earliest two glassworks, one of which predated Birmingham's canal system, were alongside a canal that carried their bulky fuel, raw materials and fragile products. At Belmont Glassworks and the Aston Flint Glassworks, both canal-side establishments, there are remains of walling and there are probably substantial below-ground remains. At the Aetna Glassworks, built off Broad Street in 1836, observations by Paul Belford during development revealed remains of glassmaking workshops and a reverbatory furnace, possibly an annealing furnace. Excavation of John Walsh Walsh's glassworks, built in 1805 on Lodge Road in Hockley, revealed the base of the brick-built cone which was 20m in diameter and had a central furnace and a flue, together with ancillary buildings and dumps of glass waste. At Belmont Glassworks the base of a small glass cone of early nineteenth century date was found, and there were more fragmentary remains of later cones.

ENERGY: COAL, PEAT, GAS, STEAM AND WATER

All Birmingham's industries used coal as a fuel by this time. Although coal seams run under Birmingham itself, they are too deep to be mined from within the city and coal had to be brought in from outside, particularly from the Black Country. A trial shaft 240ft (72m) deep was dug in 1846 in Bartley Green in an attempt to mine coal for the brick and tile industry here, but it proved unsuccessful. Its spoil heap survives, together with brickwork of the housing of a steam pumping engine and the pond from which the engine obtained its water. Hamstead Colliery just outside the city, and mining coal under it, was in operation between 1875 and 1965. Coal was carried from it along a tramway which ran over the River Tame, through the grounds of Hamstead Hall. A short-lived coal mine near the River Tame in Perry Barr was out of use before the end of the nineteenth century.

Although coal and, to a lesser extent, wood were used as domestic fuels, peat was also dug for fuel on a small scale. Peat up to 1m deep in the Longmoor Valley in Sutton Park was dug from the Old Peat Pit, a hollow running at right angles to the Longmoor Brook, in the eighteenth century and presumably earlier. There are also former peat pits near Longmoor Pool.

145

Coal gas provided a new source of light and heat in the early nineteenth century. The fortuitous discovery of the well-preserved retort house, retort house extension and coal store of Birmingham's first gasworks in Gas Street when demolition and redevelopment was proposed was followed by documentary research by Toni Demidowicz. The gasworks was established in 1818. The retort house surviving today was built in 1822, and an extension and a coal store were added to it six years later. Coal was heated in retorts, cylindrical metal vessels laid horizontally, to produce gas, which was piped through lime to purify it, and stored in gas holders. Tar was extracted from the gas as a by-product and coke remaining after gas had been removed from coal was retained and sold.

Detailed recording of the above ground remains by the then Royal Commission on Historical Monuments and Steve Linnane, and excavations and observations by John Halsted and Steve Litherland preceding and during renovation of the structures and development of the adjoining land have revealed many details about the site. There was originally a single-arched opening between each part of the L-shaped retort house. One side of the retort house was originally open, and its roof was supported on this side by a row of cast-iron columns that were later encased in brickwork to form a series of arches. The columns rested on a brick footing incorporated semicircular arches, probably the retort bases. At the top of the colonnade, a canopy extended 3m from it, covering the coke taken from the retorts. There was a slot for the horizontal support for the canopy in each cast iron column.

To the south of the retort house, a rectangular brick tank containing coal tar residue was found, together with a row of three gasholders and a fourth to the west. The gasholders were cylindrical brick structures which contained water through which the gas was bubbled and were capped by a cover held in place by a timber frame supported by four vertical posts. Excavation revealed the brickwork of the row of three gasholders, which were 16.4m (55ft 4in) to 17.3m (58ft 8in) in diameter, clay around the outer face of the brickwork to prevent leakage of the water they contained, and the bases of the timber posts supporting the framework over them *(86)*. The gasholders had been constructed on the existing ground level on what was a steeply sloping site and the ground was then built up around them.

The Gas Street gasworks was supplied with coal from a canal basin running alongside it. A second gasworks was built between Fazeley Street and the Warwick Canal in 1836 *(87)*. Its retort house, a rectangular hall like that at Gas Street, survives to full height but has a later roof. There was formerly a wharf adjoining the retort house, and a projecting wing housed the gasworks smithy. The gas holders and lime purifiers were in a yard and beyond this there was a row of buildings along the Fazeley Street frontage of which the former meter house, offices and dwelling house survive.

86 The base of a gas holder at the gasworks in Gas Street. The square brick arrangement in the right foreground holds the remains of a timber from the framework over the gasholder

87 Fazeley Street Gasworks on the Warwick Canal. The retort house is the right-hand of the twin gables in the foreground. The gas holders were in the yard to its right. The canal crosses the River Rea near the gasworks

Coal was the fuel used to produce steam, which was used to power Birmingham's industries from the late eighteenth century but was not a major source of power in Birmingham until the 1830s and '40s. Up until then, there had been a greater reliance on manpower and water power. Although there is an especial association of Birmingham with steam power through Boulton and Watt, few engines designed by them were actually used in Birmingham, and parts for their engines were made at Soho Foundry in nearby Smethwick. Most of the evidence for the use of steam engines in Birmingham is from documentary sources, and no Birmingham steam engine survives in its original location, but there are remains of engine houses and associated features. The engine house and pond at Bartley Green have been described above and the drive shaft tunnel at the Soho Manufactory site is described below. Steam engines were used to pump water onto the canal system. The lower part of the housing for a pumping engine installed in 1812 survives on the Digbeth Branch canal at Ashted, near the site of the Belmont Glassworks. The engine house was built on a slope down to the canal and the ground within and behind it has been raised up to form a level surface. Excavations revealed details inside the pumping station including the pump shaft, sandstone slabs that held the support for the engine's beam, and a pit that held the engine's condenser tank. These are similar to those found in excavation of the Smethwick Engine site just outside Birmingham, whose engine is displayed in the Thinktank at Millennium Point. The steam engine originally at Ashted also survives, not in Birmingham but in the Henry Ford Museum in Dearborn, Michigan, United States, together with another Boulton and Watt canal pumping engine of 1795 originally at Bowyer Street. The two engines demonstrate the developing design over 20 years. The Bowyer Street engine is the earlier type, with a large oak beam like that at Smethwick, while the Ashted engine has a narrower cast iron beam.

Some of Birmingham's many watermills originated as corn mills and were later converted for industrial use, and others were newly built in the post medieval period as corn mills or specifically for industrial processes such as sharpening, grinding and polishing metal products and cloth fulling. As with Birmingham's earlier mills, documentary research and fieldwork by George Demidowicz and Ken Williams has revealed much detail about known mills and has located some previously unrecognised sites. Buildings survive at only a few of these but the pools, dams, head races and tail races still visible at many sites are substantial pieces of water engineering. Head races extracted water from a river or stream at a higher level than the mill to provide a head of water, and tail races returned it at a lower level.

The head race at New Hall Mill is a small canal on an embankment that runs parallel to Plants Brook to take water from 700m upstream into the mill pool, which is really just a widening of the head race. The date of the head race is unknown. New Hall Mill was built by 1586, but not necessarily on

88 The River Cole and the tailrace of Trittiford Mill

the same site as the existing mill, because a low-lying area at the upstream end of the head race may have been the site of an earlier mill pool and mill. The oldest part of the existing buildings has a stone-built round storey which would have supported timber-framed upper storeys. Reused timbers in the later range, including middle crucks and beams with mortice slots may be from the earlier building. A bulge in the bank of the present mill pond indicates a later increase in size. On the other side of the city, races for Hurst Mill in King's Norton and Wychall run alongside the River Rea and the eighteenth-century head and tail races for Trittiford Mill and Sarehole Mill run parallel to the River Cole for 1½ miles *(88)*. Another of Trittiford's head races, taking water from the Chinn Brook to its west, survives as a slight hollow running almost parallel to but upslope from the stream. Trittiford Mill was built shortly before 1783. Sarehole Mill was given permission to construct a new head race from the River Cole in 1768. The mill was built in the sixteenth century and in addition to its adjacent pool its water was also provided from a pool in what is now Moseley Bog. This was drained in the middle of the nineteenth century but its dam still survives. A pond at one end of the dam occupies part of the quarry from which the material for the dam was dug. The dam curves round slightly at each end to enclose the end of the pool. Pebbles on its surface may have been deliberately laid to stabilise it, and short stretches of brick walls held a sluice to control the flow of water through it.

Sutton Park's eighteenth-century mills at Longmoor, Powells and Blackroot were all powered by a mill pool which was created by damming a stream, without any head races, and in each case there is a quarry at one end of the dam. The sixteenth century Blade Mill in Sutton Park was powered by a long head race, surviving as a dry hollow, running from a now-drained mill pool 250m away.

Much of the machinery of a water mill was at basement level, and excavations and recording at several sites have shown how much survives below ground even where the buildings have disappeared. At Wychall Mill Anthony Martin revealed the wheel pit and timber machinery bases of the nineteenth-century mill, and excavations at Edgbaston Mill revealed the wheel pits and head race of the eighteenth-century mill. At Northfield Mill the waterwheel pit, pit-wheel pit and axle pit were found and recorded, and the height of the water inlet channel in the surviving mill pool wall enabled the wheel diameter to be estimated at 4.5m. Brick-built tunnels carrying the tail race of Lifford Mill survive under Lifford Hall. George Demidowicz's detailed recording of the surviving substructure at Hill Hook Mill showed several phases. The earliest change was to accommodate a larger water wheel, and there were subsequent changes in the layout of the mill machinery.

The Soho Manufactory

The Soho Manufactory was established by Mathew Boulton in 1761. He was attracted to the site because there was already an energy source: a water mill powered by a pool fed from Hockley Brook. Boulton introduced a steam engine to the site not to drive machinery directly but to pump water back to the wheel of the rolling and polishing mill. This was the only source of power in the manufactory complex until 1788, when a steam engine was introduced to cut and polish coin blanks. A range of metal products was produced at the site, including plated ware, buttons, buckles and coins and medals in a mint. All of the buildings on the site were demolished in the 1850s and 1860s, and the site is now occupied by houses and their gardens and small factories. The results of excavations here are a good example of the contribution that archaeological investigation can make to our understanding of a well-documented industrial site, and at the same time demonstrate how much might survive below ground even when there are few or no above-ground remains.

Detailed documentary research by George Demidowicz enabled him to compile a detailed plan and reconstruction drawing of the manufactory and mint. Excavations identified the locations of some of these buildings on the ground and also located features that were mentioned in documents but not shown on plans. Foundations of the front wall of the principal building and a cellar were found under a present factory forecourt. These had been covered and filled with rubble from the building's demolition in the middle of the nineteenth century. The foundations of the mint building, discovered in what is now a garden, included a pit that may have contained a machine. This contained copper coin blanks and a Sumatran coin of 1803. Nearby there was a brick tunnel, which had originally contained a drive shaft. Written records show that this was constructed in 1824-26 but its location was not shown on any plans. The tunnel was also located at other points on the site, together with another tunnel at right angles to it which led to the site of a steam engine.

Walls of the coin cutting out room were found under a patio. The room was in part of a crescent-shaped building in which latchets (removable shoe buckles) were made in the late eighteenth and early nineteenth century, before it was incorporated into the mint. Further excavations located the junction between the square end building of this range and the curving main part of it, and another section of the drive shaft tunnel.

MOVING THINGS AROUND — TRANSPORT

As in previous periods, industrial raw materials, fuels, and goods and products for domestic consumption were coming into Birmingham from very local sources, such as agricultural produce, from slightly further afield such as coal and pottery, and, via England's ports, from overseas. Direct and indirect archaeological evidence shows that more exotic goods were reaching Birmingham from the sixteenth century onwards than at any time since the Roman period.

Wednesbury, the source of Birmingham's coal, probably also supplied much of the pottery in everyday use in the seventeenth century. By the eighteenth and nineteenth centuries, pottery produced in Stoke-on-Trent was in use not only in the city centre but also at a farm in Saltley. Pottery from continental Europe was being used in the city centre and at the wealthier houses of rural Birmingham in the sixteenth and seventeenth centuries. French sixteenth-century Martincamp pottery has been found in Edgbaston Street, hard fired German stoneware pottery made in Siegburg, Frechen and Cologne in the sixteenth century has been found at Park Street, Edgbaston Street and Birmingham Moat, sixteenth-century Mediterranean majolica at Moor Street and Weoley Castle, and a seventeenth-century Westerwald mug at Park Street. Excavations at Sandwell Priory showed that a range of imported pottery was being used in the house occupying the site in the sixteenth to early eighteenth centuries. A Spanish olive jar was found in a post-medieval deposit at Park Street, where there were also seeds of grapes and figs. The sixteenth-century barrel of French wood reused to store lime on Floodgate Street must have arrived in Birmingham containing wine, and further evidence of wine consumption is provided by wine bottles. American tobacco was smoked in the many clay pipes found from the seventeenth century onwards, and a seed of thorn apple, a North American tree with medicinal properties, was found at Park Street. Seeds or saplings were also brought in to grow trees native to North America in the grounds of Sandwell Hall, such as the swamp cypress alongside one of its pools. Shell used to make buttons in the city centre came from the Middle or Far East.

Before the middle of the eighteenth century everything that was brought into Birmingham, whatever its origin, would have been carried along roads or tracks. Birmingham's first artificial waterway, completed in 1769, was constructed to carry coal from Wednesbury. Canals transported fuel, raw materials and finished products for Birmingham's industries and became foci for industrial development. They are accompanied by features such as basins, wharves and the sites of steam-powered pumping engines like that at Ashted described above. In addition to these, and particularly striking to an archaeologist, there are the often under-appreciated earthworks of the canal system constructed to create a relatively level course and avoid locks and therefore water loss: cuttings, embankments, tunnels and their spoil heaps.

Cuttings and embankments for canals are the equivalent of modern motorway earthworks. The Tame Valley Canal, completed in 1844 and therefore postdating most of the railway system, runs in a deep cutting through Tower Hill in Perry Barr. At Minworth, an embankment carries the Birmingham and Fazeley Canal, opened in 1789, across the broad valley of Hurst Brook *(89)*. Canal tunnels have left their mark above ground as lines of mounds representing earth carried up shafts during the tunnel's construction, such as the Lapal Tunnel which carried the Dudley no.2 Canal, constructed in 1797-98 under what is now Woodgate Valley Country Park, and The Mounds in King's Norton over a tunnel carrying the Worcester Canal under Wast Hills.

The water supply to canals involved the construction of reservoirs such as Edgbaston and feeders such as that constructed in 1811 across fields now forming King's Norton recreation ground. The canal system was imposed on a developed landscape. Canals paid little heed to some features but had to respect rights of way. At Minworth Greaves the Birmingham and Fazeley Canal cut across ridge and furrow (now levelled by ploughing), which corresponded to strips in the open field, but just beyond the city boundary Broad Balk Bridge had to be provided to allow access along unploughed edges or balks into the fields.

Like canals, railways are often accompanied by major engineering works such as embankments, cuttings and viaducts. Excavation has shown the extent of earthmoving involved in railway construction and the resulting changes in the city's topography. At the junction of Park Street and Bordesley Street Nick

89 The Birmingham and Fazeley Canal running on an embankment at Minwort

Tavener's excavation showed that a former ground surface containing seven-teenth- and eighteenth-century pottery was covered by over 2m of earth which was derived from the adjoining railway cutting. At Curzon Street a sloping site was cut into to form a level area for a goods yard; the garden or orchard remains buried by levelling for the goods yard are described below. Stables and other buildings belonging to the goods yard were recorded in detail before their demolition to make way for the new Millennium Point. The earliest building dated to 1842. It was accompanied by a purpose-built stable of 1881-88, which was an L-shaped building divided into individual stalls, each with a feeding rack and with an elaborate foul drainage system in which liquid waste was chan-nelled from the first floor into hollow cast iron columns supporting the floor. The stall divisions did not reach the full height of the horses, but in one wing brick partitions were later constructed to fully segregate the stalls and isolate individual horses, enabling it to function as a sanatorium.

CITY LIVING: HOUSES AND GARDENS

In addition to the remains of past industries, excavation and detailed recording of historic buildings has also thrown some light on what it was like to live in what is now the city centre and inner city areas between the sixteenth and nineteenth centuries.

In the Bull Ring area, pottery, industrial debris and environmental evidence show segregation into domestic and industrial zones and fluctuations in the social status of the sites. The seventeenth- and eighteenth-century pits containing industrial debris at Park Street have been described above. Building rubble in the infill of some of the pits indicates clearance of houses and their replacement. By the early eighteenth century there were grand houses with their gardens on the street frontage, with workshops behind them. Pits containing seeds of cypress, poplar, rose, plum, strawberry, beet and turnip show what trees, flowers, fruit and vegetables were grown there. Flowers and shrubs would have been kept in pots, remains of which were found on the site, and the manufacture of flowerpots at Floodgate Street shows that there was some demand for them. Similarly at Edgbaston Street large houses occupied the street frontage: the pits near the frontage and tanning pits further back were filled in during the early eighteenth century. A humic soil here may represent the garden immediately behind the house, but similar deposits at Park Street and Moor Street may indicate periods when land was vacant and possibly used for market gardening. At both Park Street and Edgbaston Street there was another change towards the end of the eighteenth century. Large quantities of pottery were thrown into the two plank-lined tanks at Park Street in about 1770, together with a finely made seventeenth-century chair, and a soil layer containing rubble was dumped or accumulated. At Edgbaston Street a group of plates and drinking vessels was thrown into a well near the frontage in the middle or late eighteenth century. Both of these might be the result of house clearance. This and the occurrence of artisans' pottery indicates a downgrading of the status of both sites as the wealthier townsfolk were moving out of the centre towards the end of the eighteenth century.

Further down the slope towards the River Rea, land reclamation in Digbeth shows that there was greater pressure on space and more intensive development. At Hartwell Smithfield Garage deliberate dumping took place in the seventeenth or eighteenth centuries over a waterlogged deposit to make it suitable for building on. At Floodgate Street next to the River Rea over 2m of material was dumped in the nineteenth century and cellars constructed through it.

A drastic change of use took place at Curzon Street in 1838 when a railway goods yard was constructed on what had previously been gardens and orchards. Excavations by Gifford and Partners revealed a cultivated soil, which was up to 60cm (2ft) thick and contained eighteenth-century pottery, under levelling for the goods yard.

Two groups of Birmingham's back-to-back houses have been recorded in detail. At Inge Street the oldest building was converted into a pair of back-to-backs by 1821 and two others were built as pairs of back-to-backs about 1830. Each is three storeys high, with a room on each floor, and originally had a cellar. The rear house of each pair faces onto an enclosed court, entered from the road frontage along a tunnel entrance. The houses facing onto the court had bay windows so that more light reached the ground floor room.

Martin Cook recorded four pairs of back-to-backs in Dudley Road that had been built in 1873 and 1874 and were therefore amongst the last to be built in the city, before the construction of back-to-backs was prohibited by a by-law in 1876. While the front and back properties of the eastern two pairs were equal and there was a through passage to the court from the frontage, the western two pairs offered superior and inferior accommodation. Their front houses were built to give the impression that they were through houses rather than back-to-backs, by providing them with access to the court behind through a short passage between them that could not be seen on the front. This would not have benefited the occupants of the rear houses, who would have had to share the passage used by the two eastern pairs for access to the road frontage.

The two cells of Aston Gaol discovered in excavations at High Street Bordesley show what life was like for miscreants. The gaol was established in the 1780s. Each cell was a subterranean brick cubicle measuring 3.4m x 2.75m with an earth floor and brick vaulted roof. Sockets in the walls show where a bench or bed would have been fixed *(90)*.

90 Excavation of a cell of Aston Gaol at High Street Bordesley

COUNTRY LIFE:
HOUSES AND GARDENS, FARMS AND FIELDS, WOODS AND SPORTS

Dating of timber-framed buildings by dendrochronology, architectural style, and in one case from a date inscribed on the building suggests that there was substantial new building or rebuilding in Birmingham and the surrounding area around 1600. An estimated felling date of 1590 was obtained by dendrochronology for timbers in Blakesley Hall and other buildings constructed in the same close-studded style in nearby West Bromwich have produced similar dates: Oak House (1604), Hill House (1601) and West Bromwich Manor House gatehouse (1591). Stratford House in Birmingham, another close-studded structure, has the date 1601 inscribed on it. The Golden Lion and Lamb House, which formerly stood in High Street Deritend and Bull Street respectively, are built in the same style as these.

Reused timber at Blakesley Hall and Oak House suggests rebuilding of an earlier structure. Blakesley Hall may originally have been moated, and excavation of the service rooms at its east end revealed a pebble surface immediately overlying natural clay and containing thirteenth-century pottery. A burnt cobbled area and burnt clay, possibly the setting for an oven, with an associated mortar floor, probably relates to the construction of the existing building in 1590 indicated by dendrochronology. These features were later replaced by a sunken brick floor with broad brick shelves, interpreted as a dairy. The eighteenth-century brick walls of a barn at Monyhull Hall in King's Norton replaced original timber walls supporting a timber roof, which was stylistically dateable to between 1550 and 1650. Crudely fitted joints suggested that the timbers had been reused, and this was confirmed by dendrochronology that showed that the roof timbers were from trees felled between 1466 and 1501.

At Sandwell Priory in West Bromwich excavation revealed well-preserved remains, which showed how the buildings of the medieval monastery had been adapted following its suppression in 1525. In about 1600 the former east range was partitioned in timber and a brick fireplace added. In the middle or later seventeenth century, brick floors replaced earth floors inside the former east range and another fireplace was installed. A timber building erected on the rubble of the demolished priory church was replaced in the later seventeenth century by a walled garden, cobbled yard and line of brick stalls At the beginning of the eighteenth century a new building, Sandwell Hall, still incorporated the former eastern range of the priory and followed its alignment but also extended to its east.

During the seventeenth and eighteenth centuries brick replaced timber as the normal building material in Birmingham and the surrounding area, although brickwork at Hay Hall in Birmingham may date to the middle of the sixteenth century, refacing an earlier timber frame. Aston Hall, the first substantial brick building in the area, was constructed between 1618 and 1635, and other brick buildings were constructed during the seventeenth century.

At Blakesley Hall, Sheldon Hall, West Bromwich Manor House and Sandwell Priory the late sixteenth- or early seventeenth-century building work took place on a site occupied in the medieval period. New brick buildings were constructed in the seventeenth century on other medieval sites in Birmingham, some of them moated like Sheldon Hall, such as Peddimore Hall and Rectory Farm in Sheldon.

The central range at Sheldon Hall is built of brick with stone dressings, and its timber roof is dated by dendrochronology to 1617-19. Recent recording by Martin Cook when previously concealed details were exposed during renovation showed that it had been inserted between two sixteenth-century wings, replacing an earlier range. The earliest surviving part is the east cross–wing, which was originally a single free-standing timber framed building with a sill beam resting on a course of stone. It stood against, or adjacent to, an earlier central range. On the west side of the original central range, the west wing was originally free-standing and its sill beam rested on the ground. Shallow grooves for wattle infill are visible only on its north and south elevations and part of its east and west, suggesting that it had additional framing added to its west and east elevations.

At Aston Hall there is no evidence for any buildings before the seventeenth century but in addition to the use of iron slag as foundations, noted above, Adrian Oswald's excavations there in 1950 revealed evidence of changes of plan during construction and alterations to the original building. Under the main entrance he found the footings of walls at oblique angles to the existing building. Foundations under floors indicated former room divisions and filled in openings had originally been constructed as oriel windows. More recently, excavations by Archaeological Investigations and Birmingham Archaeology have revealed former walls and buildings around the great house and shown how the garden terraces were constructed. In front of the house, discovery of the footings of a wall joining two lodges confirms that the house was originally entered through a courtyard, as shown on a seventeenth-century drawing (91). The types of brick and mortar used in the wall are identical to those used in the main house, showing that they are contemporary. The excavation also showed that the entrance into this courtyard had been narrowed at a later stage. The Stable Court to the north of the main house was another courtyard with the stable on the east, which still survives, and another range on its north which was demolished in the nineteenth century. Excavation of the former north range has revealed remains of the brewhouse, bakehouse, laundry, a cellar and an icehouse. Trenches through garden terraces showed that they had been created by dumping soil on the existing surfaces. The soil came from the park further away from the house, where excavations revealed earth had been scraped away.

91 Footings of the former wall across the courtyard at Aston Hall

The existing Witton Hall was constructed in about 1730, possibly replacing an earlier building on the same site. It is a plain rectangular building but lacks the symmetry expected for a building of this period. A straight joint on the ground floor, extending just up to the level of the base of the ground floor windows, shows that there was a change of plan when building had progressed this far. The main building, a single room deep, may originally have been intended to have a projecting wing at one end, forming an L-shape partly enclosing a courtyard. This plan was abandoned during construction and the main building was extended to the east, becoming two rooms deep. Its main entrance, on the south, was probably originally approached up steps and had an elaborate door frame which was later reset in the west side. Eighteenth-century maps show rectangular and oval ponds on two sides of the building, extending to its south to enclose a garden. In addition to one of the ponds, excavations revealed a cobbled yard and eighteenth- and nineteenth-century garden features *(92)*. These were dated by pottery contained in them, but none of them were shown on historic maps or mentioned in documents. They included ditches and gullies at right angles to each other, which provided drainage, or served as boundaries by themselves or accompanied by hedges. Some of these may have been the boundaries of fields that were on the site before the garden was created in the eighteenth century, and were subsequently incorporated into it. The garden layout was modified in the early nineteenth century. In addition to the line of a fence around the pools and possible planting pits for trees or shrubs, the excavations revealed details of garden design. On the edge of the largest pool and within the fenced area, there were gullies surrounding two square or U-shaped features, one of them about 10m square. These may have been gazebos, built in timber and resting on timber ground beams or shallow brick or stone plinths, which had been removed when the buildings themselves had been demolished. On the other side of the pond from these, three square mortared bases may have supported statues. The early nineteenth-century features were short-lived; the gullies were filled in with demolition rubble and the ponds filled in.

The estates of Hamstead Hall and Moseley Hall each contained an icehouse, constructed in the eighteenth century. These structures were used to store ice derived from a nearby stretch of water which was then taken as required to the Hall to cool food and drinks. They consist of a storage chamber with a domed roof, whose lower part is cylindrical or tapering and extends below ground level. The chamber is entered along a passage and both passage and chamber are covered with an earth mound to provide insulation. The entrance faces north and there is often a tree on or next to the mound to provide shade. The Moseley icehouse lies near a pool, the source of its ice, and Chris Patrick's observation during renovation work showed that it was entered along a brick path and there was a brick wall to hold back the mound on each side of it. A passage turns at right angles from the entrance to lead originally through one or two further doors to the storage chamber. The chamber is about 10ft (3m) in diameter and was probably originally 14ft (4.2m) high. The icehouse belonging to Hamstead hall lies near the River Tame and was constructed about 1776. The domed storage chamber is 10ft (3m) in diameter and has a

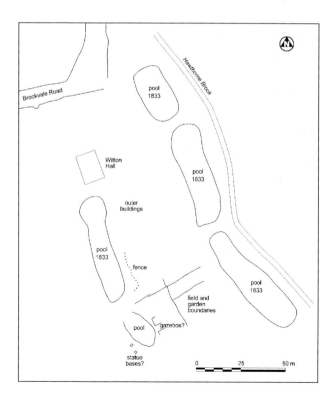

92 Witton Hall and its grounds. Incorporating information on plans by Warwickshire Museum Field Services

93 Base of the icehouse belonging to Hamstead Hall

cavity wall at the base of the dome. It was entered along a passageway from the north *(93)*. Drawings and measurements made in the 1930s before the dome collapsed and the lower part of the storage chamber was partly filled in show that the base of the storage chamber was 7ft (2.1m) below the entrance into it from the passage, and the height of the storage chamber from the base to the top of the dome was 14ft 6in (4.3m). Another icehouse, at Holders Lane, originally belonging to Moor End House, is visible only as a mound.

The Hamstead icehouse is almost identical in form and size to that belonging to Sandwell Hall about 1½ miles away and both are almost certainly the work of the same builder. Another feature in the estates of both Sandwell and Hamstead is a heated garden wall containing flues within its thickness which carried the heat from an adjoining fire, so that fruit trees could be grown against it. The one at Hamstead is the south wall of a walled garden that is shown on a map of 1794. The garden's polygonal plan follows the line of the moat around Hamstead Hall's medieval predecessor near the River Tame.

At Aston, Moseley and Hamstead the parkland around the country houses has been encroached upon to such an extent that it is difficult to appreciate its original size, appearance and contents, but at Sandwell, just outside the city, the eighteenth-century landscape can still be appreciated through surviving and excavated remains even though Sandwell Hall itself, the home of the Earls of Dartmouth, was demolished in 1928. The park is bounded by a stone

94 Wall of an eighteenth-century farm building in Saltley

wall on the east and a brick wall on the south, where there is also an entrance arch. An avenue of sweet chestnut trees leads up to the hall from the east, and a ha-ha ran along the east and north sides of the hall. To the west of the icehouse mentioned above, another ice house, a menagerie and an orangery lay within an area bounded by a ditch, partly waterfilled, around pools which were originally medieval fishponds. The enclosed area and islands in the pools also contained exotic trees brought from North America. Beyond the enclosed area there is a home farm with a walled garden.

A farm building marked on a map of 1760 was excavated in Saltley *(94)*. It was brick-built and contained at least three rooms, two of which had brick floors and the third had water-worn cobbles. Under the cobbles there was clay infilling for a former shallow cellar, which contained much pottery, probably all deposited at once in about 1780. The pottery consists mainly of tablewares and contains types produced from about 1720 onwards. It is dominated by blackwares and there are also creamwares including a cup with ornate twisted handles, a black basalt ware teapot from Wedgwood's Etruria works, and pearlwares. The pottery is very similar in both date and type to that thrown into a timber-lined pit at Park Street in the city centre. It shows that by this time fine mass-produced pottery was widely available and widely used. As at Park Street, the pottery was thrown away either as part of a house clearance, possibly resulting from a change of ownership. The Saltley building was not a dwelling but its brick-floored rooms may have been part of a dairy, like that at Blakesley Hall, described above. Excavation of Longbridge House and Longbridge Farm revealed the footings of eighteenth-century brick and sandstone buildings, and barns at Peddimore and Langley Heath Farm were dated to the eighteenth century by dendrochronology.

Ridge and furrow was used as a cultivation method into the nineteenth century. In contrast to the broad curving medieval ridge and furrow, later ridge and furrow is characteristically straight and narrow. Much of the ridge and furrow in what are now Birmingham's public parks – such as Highbury Park and Cannon Hill Park – is probably eighteenth or nineteenth century in date and results from cultivation of the fields from which the parks were created.

Former open fields were divided into smaller hedged and ditched fields from the later medieval period onwards. In Northfield, some of these early enclosures near the River Rea contain ridge and furrow 4.5m to 5m wide with a slight C-shaped curve. Excavations at Peddimore in Sutton Coldfield revealed field boundary ditches created in the eighteenth or nineteenth centuries.

A low mound that overlies ridge and furrow on Hodge Hill Common is probably a pillow mound (an artificial rabbit warren); a rare survivor in Birmingham of evidence for one use of the extensive open common land in Birmingham, some of it heathland, in the eighteenth century. In the later eighteenth and early nineteenth centuries most of this land was enclosed into separate fields which were straight-sided, rectangular or square, and bounded by hawthorn hedges, and new straight roads were constructed. Because the land had not previously been cultivated, earlier features survived and influenced the alignment of the new fields, such as the ditch of a Roman enclosure at Langley Mill Farm, which is followed by the new nineteenth-century boundary and must therefore have been visible when the latter was laid out (23). Much of the land brought into cultivation was found to be poor soil and was eventually built over, but extensive enclosure landscapes survive along Hillwood Common Road and just outside the city on the slopes of Barr Beacon.

Sutton Park contains remains of post-medieval woodland management and its nineteenth century recreational use. Much of its woodland was managed as coppice from the sixteenth century onwards and was surrounded by banks and ditches, originally with hedges or fences on top of the banks, to exclude grazing animals. Virtually all of these boundaries survive, showing that the extent of the woodland enclosed in the sixteenth century corresponds closely to subdivisions of the medieval deer park and that these subdivisions them-selves protected woodland. Spectator banks surround part of an oval racecourse where horse races were held in the 1840s. The greens of a nineteenth-century golf course are still visible as flat areas and one of the bunkers survives as a prominent pit.

DEATH IN EIGHTEENTH- AND NINETEENTH-CENTURY BIRMINGHAM

Other than the unexpected burials at Park Street, described above, we see Birmingham people themselves in the archaeological record for the first time in the eighteenth century. At St Martin's and St Philip's in the city centre and Holy Trinity in Sutton Coldfield, eighteenth- and nineteenth-century burials provide evidence for living conditions and attitudes to death.

Burials took place at St Martin's from the twelfth century to the middle of the nineteenth century. It was a relatively small churchyard, and was extended in the later eighteenth century. The northern side of the churchyard was excavated in 2001 *(95)*. Most of the burials that survived intact and could be dated belonged to the nineteenth century. A few burials dated to the eighteenth century or earlier, and the earliest datable burial, from lettering on the coffin lid, was of 1720. There was much intercutting and much disarticulated bone, some of which had been collected up into charnel pits. The total of 857 burials of mainly late eighteenth and early nineteenth-century date makes St Martin's the largest group of excavated burials of this period in Britain other than Spitalfields in London. The majority of burials were in earth-cut graves, some containing double or multiple burials. There were also 35 vaults, in which coffins were placed on separate floors to prevent crushing, and brick shafts in which there was floor space for one coffin only and coffins had therefore to be stacked separated by timber supports. One vault was more elaborate than the others and consisted of chambers approached along a passage.

95 Excavations in St Martin's churchyard

As might be expected, there was high infant mortality and there were several infant burials, some alongside their mother indicating her death at or soon after giving birth. Skeletons of adults showed diseases like arthritis, and healed broken bones indicated injuries caused by accidents or violence. The top of the skull of some individuals had been cut off to examine the brain in an autopsy, and replaced before burial. In addition to skeletal remains, hair, clothing, plant remains and coffins survived at St Martin's. Nitrogen isotopes in hair indicate the consumption of high quantities of freshwater fish or of pigs. The latter is probably more likely in an inland urban area like Birmingham, where pigs would be kept in backyards. Birmingham was famous as a market for pigs. One burial was accompanied by woollen stockings. There was a legal requirement to use only wool in burials from the late seventeenth century to the early nineteenth century. There were wool mix textiles in the mid-nineteenth-century burials and linen-effect wool, possibly achieved through chemical treatment. Fastening pins showed that burials had been covered with shrouds and winding sheets.

Silk was used to line the coffins buried in vaults, i.e. the higher status burials, and wool for the others. The well-preserved plant remains, mostly leaves, were from wreaths and floral offerings. Box, traditionally associated with burials, was the most common, and there were also juniper, a medicinal plant, cherry and privet. The coffins were predominantly made of elm but oak and other species were used. There was no class distinction in coffin timber: elm was used in coffins in vaults as well as in earth graves. The main coffin structure would need planks from mature trees. Both elm and oak are slow-growing trees and therefore the large number of coffins had major implications for woodland resources.

Coffin 'furniture', the grips and grip plates for coffins and coffin plates, was manufactured in Birmingham from the middle of the eighteenth century and was part of the cast metal industry. In earth-cut graves, the grips and grip plates were cast iron, but burials in brick-lined graves and vaults had copper alloy grips and plates of copper alloy and other materials. Coffin plates were brass, and brass tacks were used to fix the cloth covering the coffin.

At St Philip's, now the cathedral, which was consecrated in 1715 and whose graveyard was in use until 1858, observation and recording during landscaping works in 2000 and 2001 confirmed the high density of burial across the whole site indicated by documentary sources. The burials included chamber vaults and brick-lined shaft graves as well as burials made in coffins alone, and there were intercutting burials. There were high levels of child mortality and diseases including rickets inevitably occurring in a growing industrial town. Tooth loss shows poor dental health and growth lines in teeth, called enamel hypoplasia, indicate stress during childhood that temporarily halted enamel formation. There was little sign of that common ailment of middle and old age, osteo-arthritis, probably because of the low life expectancy: many of the excavated individuals were young adults. Low life expectancy and health problems are in marked contrast to the grand buildings constructed in this part of Birmingham in the eighteenth and nineteenth centuries.

St Phillip's burial ground was reduced in size in the eighteenth century by the construction of roads around it, which covered earlier burials. At Park Street, where the nineteenth century overspill burial ground for St Martin's is crossed by Albert Street, burials revealed in a service trench included an amputee.

A small excavation in 1992 in the graveyard of Holy Trinity, Sutton Coldfield's medieval parish church, revealed no surviving medieval burials. The earliest probably dated to the middle of the eighteenth century, and the density of eighteenth- and nineteenth-century burials was such as to have destroyed remains of earlier periods. Again as at St Martin's, burials were intercut. The bone was in poor condition because of acid soils. There were some copper or tin alloy coffin plates with embossed or impressed decoration, mostly badly corroded. The graveyard was extended to the west in 1832, and burials were made over the former boundary.

BIRMINGHAM AT WAR

The archaeological remains relating to armed conflict in the nineteenth and twentieth centuries include trenches, targets and a campsite for military training in Sutton Park, a munitions factory in Witton, an anti-aircraft gun base, pillboxes, air raid shelters and a blast-proof Cold War bunker.

The western side of Sutton Park was used for military training from the nineteenth century. The remains of targets for a rifle range constructed in 1881 consist of a concrete lined trench in which soldiers marking the targets sheltered and a mound behind it to catch stray shot (96). The soldiers' camp site was at the other end of the range where in an area about 45m(150ft) square the locations of at least ten bell tents are marked by the drainage trenches dug around them, which are each about 8in (20cm) wide and 9in deep, and surround a circular area 13 to 15ft (4.3m) in diameter. To their west, another trench surrounds an oval area 54 x 23ft (16.4 x 7m), possibly a marquee. On a slope to the east of the range, near Longmoor Brook, there is a zigzag practice trench. Excavations nearby on what was thought to be a prehistoric barrow but proved to be natural mound located a straight sided vertical trench, probably military, and a large posthole, possibly to hold a flagpole whose flag indicated when manoeuvres were in progress. Angular ditches near Bracebridge Pool are probably also military practice trenches.

The Lion Works in Witton was established in 1862 to manufacture munitions. The buildings and structures on the site, consisting of filling sheds, explosives stores or magazines, a railway, a covered firing range, a pill box and an air-raid shelter were recorded by Dan Slatcher in 2003 before they were

cleared for new development. The site has been in continuous use since 1862 so has been modified over time to meet different requirements of the industry. The earliest surviving structures date from the First World War to 1925 and some are marked on a plan of the site of 1916. Datum plaques of 1916 on one filling shed and one magazine confirm that they existed at this date. The site layout was designed to isolate any explosion and individual buildings were designed to release the blast force. The filling sheds, dating from the First World War, were long single storey buildings with timber long walls and brick end walls. The magazines were timber sheds surrounded by earth mounds about 2m high and 6m thick and approached by wooden walkways. Some of magazines were in positions marked on the 1916 plan. A light railway served the magazines. The firing range was largely enclosed and divided into individual butts. A semi-underground brick air-raid shelter and a square pillbox were built at the Lion Works during the Second World War.

As well as those serving individual workplaces and individual dwellings, air-raid shelters were provided at publicly accessible buildings such as pubs; for example at the Albion Inn in Sheepcote Street in the city centre where a cellar reinforced to serve as an air-raid shelter was recorded by Kirsty Nichol. It was subdivided by brick walls supporting reinforced concrete blocks strengthening the ceiling, and could be entered from within the building or direct from the street.

One of the anti-aircraft gun installations protecting Birmingham was at Hilltop in Handsworth, on high ground overlooking the city from the north-west. Each of the two octagonal gun pits contain sockets for the gun's securing

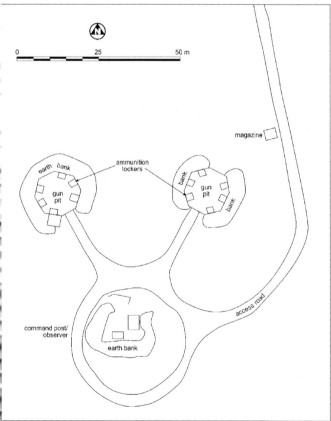

96 *Opposite* Targets in Sutton Park, showing the concrete-lined trenches and the mound behind them

97 *Above* Gun pit at Hilltop anti-aircraft gun installation. The gun mounting is in the centre with ammunition lockers around it, and the whole structure is surrounded by an earth bank

98 *Left* Plan of Hilltop anti-aircraft gun emplacement. *Based on the Ordnance Survey map and reproduced by permission of Ordnance Survey on behalf of the Controller of Her Majesty's Stationery Office, © Crown Copyright 100042011*

bolts, set in a concrete base and surrounded by six concrete ammunition lockers, in turn surrounded by earth banks *(97)*. There is a concrete access road to each gun pit from a group of buildings also surrounded by earth banks forming the command post, which would have included a sighting telescope. A brick magazine adjoins the access road beyond the command post *(98)*.

Pill boxes and other structures were built to counteract invasion. A pill box now regrettably lost to new development overlooked Birmingham Airport which had been requisitioned for military use during the Second World War. It was a concrete-built irregular hexagon. Canals were seen as possible access routes by an invasion force, particularly if road blocking was successful. On the Worcester Canal at Lifford in Kings Norton, a pillbox was constructed from a concrete pipe set on its end, with slits cut in it. A further two lengths of pipe were added on top to make the structure look like an industrial chimney. A brick structure alongside the Digbeth Branch Canal near Ashted Tunnel, is a small air raid shelter with a baffle entrance to protect against blast. Nearby there was a cleansing station or decontamination unit to treat people affected by anticipated chemical and gas attacks. Another defensive structure, brick with a concrete roof, is on the top of a garden wall at the junction of Harrisons Road and Richmond Hill Road in Edgbaston. During the Cold War, a blast proof semi-subterranean anti-aircraft operations room was built in St Bernard's Road in Sutton Coldfield.

INTO MODERN BIRMINGHAM

The wide range of archaeological remains of the past few centuries hark back to an even earlier Birmingham on the one hand and describe the emergence of a major industrial town and its rural surroundings on the other. They bring us up to the radical changes wrought on the appearance of the city centre and other parts of the city since the middle of the twentieth century.

CHAPTER 6
INTO THE FUTURE

Finally, we can highlight some gaps in our knowledge of particular periods of Birmingham's past and suggest how they might be answered, and identify some common themes across various periods. We consider how Birmingham's archaeological remains are protected for the future and how they are explained to those who live in, work in or visit the city.

SOME QUESTIONS AND SOME COMMON THEMES

Although there is at least some archaeological evidence from Birmingham for each period division of the past, some periods are still very poorly represented. Although it might be thought futile to expect more discoveries of the very earliest periods, deposits containing Palaeolithic material probably survive and Mesolithic and Neolithic flint debris has been found in fieldwalking in far greater quantities than the relatively few Neolithic and Bronze Age axes and other objects that have been found by chance, therefore settlements of this period may be discovered in the future. More burnt mounds are likely to be discovered, since they are distinctive, moderately visible and can be observed and recorded even in relatively poor conditions. More information on the function of these sites will be provided by associated features that are less archaeologically visible and may be at some distance from the mound. These may also include the places where the people using the mounds lived. It is therefore important that the areas surrounding burnt mounds are investigated as well as the burnt mounds themselves.

The archaeological evidence shows that, despite assertions to the contrary, there is no reason why the population density and number of settlements in Birmingham in the prehistoric and Roman periods should have been less than anywhere else in the country. One of Birmingham's Iron Age settlements has been found and more will undoubtedly be discovered, possibly, like the Langley Mill Farm site, in close proximity to Roman features. There are potentially a large number of Roman settlement sites in the area. Much Roman pottery has probably been found in gardens in modern residential areas but has not been recognised as old by its finders because of the large quantities of modern debris and the expectation that everything they might find is therefore of recent date. Both of the known Roman pottery kiln sites in the area were chance discoveries. There are likely to have been more roadside settlements like that at Longdales Road, since the imposed network of roads must have influenced the location and character of civilian settlements. In the absence of a major settlement within Birmingham in the Roman period, places outside it would have determined, or at least influenced, the economy of rural settlements.

The Anglo-Saxon period is currently as sparsely represented archaeologically in Birmingham as the far more distant Palaeolithic, and discussion of the period is largely speculation, like that for the city centre, or assumption, like the notion that at least some of the medieval villages that are now city suburbs have at least late Saxon origins. While this may be the case, the elusive Anglo-Saxon sites might equally be sought near known Roman or medieval farmsteads, particularly where they themselves are close together.

Beyond the living and their settlements, where were Birmingham's dead buried in all periods before the Middle Ages? Only one possible burial site, Kingstanding Mound, is so far known in Birmingham for this long period. People using burnt mounds may have buried their dead in or near their settlements, wherever they are, and the dead of the Roman settlements may have been buried alongside roads. Burials of all periods up to the Middle Ages may have been on or near territorial boundaries. Most but not all medieval and later burials will be in churchyards, but because these have continued in use into the nineteenth or even twentieth centuries, the earliest burials do not survive intact, as at St Martin's in the city centre and Holy Trinity in Sutton Coldfield. However, there may be surviving medieval burials inside churches, particularly where the building has been extended over the former graveyard, or immediately adjoining the church.

It is easy to assume that the medieval landscape is relatively well known but this is only true in general terms. Many houses of apparently later date, particularly farmhouses and barns, may have medieval origins, in some cases indicated by documentary references, and incorporate medieval remains. The survival of below-ground archaeological remains of medieval village houses has been demonstrated in Kings Norton but similar remains of a town house have yet to be found in either Birmingham or Sutton Coldfield. No structural remains of medieval water mills have yet been found, and their relationship to later mill buildings and watercourses on the same site is unknown, but there are several sites where their remains are likely to survive. No archaeological evidence of the crafts and industries that must have taken place in rural areas has yet been identified, other than the gullies at Walkers Heath.

Careful observation of buildings is likely to show that several earlier buildings survive behind later frontages than are known as yet. Detailed structural analysis may also reveal hitherto unknown phases of the building and sometimes changes in use. The value of dendrochronology for surviving buildings and excavated structures of the medieval and post-medieval periods has been amply demonstrated. Although not all buildings will have suitable timbers, sampling and dating timber buildings and timber roofs of post-medieval brick buildings will refine assumed architectural dating. It will provide more information on the extent of apparent new building or rebuilding about 1600, and on the earliest uses of brick in Birmingham. Excavation of abandoned post-medieval buildings such as that at Saltley can provide information not only on the structure but also allow comparison of lifestyles, represented by pottery and other objects, between sites.

The number and extent of Birmingham's apparently rather limited natural resources has been under-appreciated. Above, or rather below, all of these is water – perhaps surprisingly for a place which is inland, does not lie on a navigable river and does not receive an exceptionally high rainfall. Water has not only been used for drinking, directly from springs or streams or via wells, but has also been engineered to serve as a status symbol in moats, for food storage in fishponds, in industrial processes such as tanning, as a power source via water mills, and as a transport link in canals to redress the lack of navigable rivers.

The solid and drift geological deposits underlying Birmingham provided a range of mineral resources. The abundant quartzite pebbles they contained proved ideal for use as miniature storage heaters in whatever processes are represented by the burnt mounds. They were used to make hand-axes in the Palaeolithic period and may have been used to make tools in other prehistoric periods, although no tools or waste material have been recognised as yet. Drift deposits and river terraces also contained flint for tool manufacture. Other minerals, sand and clay, were used for metalworking for which Birmingham is well known and for its now less appreciated brick, tile and pottery industries.

Like pottery making, leather tanning is another industry that is not normally associated with Birmingham now, despite its importance in the past. One of its major requirements, water, was available locally, but its hides came from the surrounding area and further afield. Fuel and raw materials that were not available in Birmingham itself were brought in from outside. The acquisition of coal, iron and lime from the Black Country from at least the thirteenth century established an important economic link in which Birmingham's development stimulated that of adjoining areas, and indeed the Black Country probably owes its industrial success to the creation of a new town in the St Martin's and Bull Ring area in the twelfth century and its subsequent growth.

Recognition of the range of industries in Birmingham from the medieval period onwards needs to be followed by a consideration of the types of structures and residues likely to survive from different industries. Distinctive structures relating to particular industries can then be recognised as surviving buildings or as excavated remains and appropriate sampling and analysis of residues can take place.

Remarkably few twentieth-century defensive sites have been recorded in Birmingham as yet. Although these sites are especially vulnerable to damage or complete destruction because of a lack of appreciation of their significance and rarity and the difficulty of finding a new use for them, there must surely be more than are currently recorded.

The specifically archaeological remains are supplemented by the related evidence for the Birmingham's past environment, ranging from beetles living in glacial conditions to seeds of plants growing in eighteenth-century gardens. There are also residues from various industrial processes. Recovery of these essential components of our understanding of the city's past will be a vital part of all future work.

Archaeological research frameworks for the West Midlands region as a whole enable us to place the archaeological evidence Birmingham in a wider context and draw attention to its significance beyond the city itself. They also highlight the requirements for detailed analysis and publication of the results of archaeological work, including that which was undertaken some years ago. Results of previous work also require reassessment in the light of current knowledge, and information from different sites needs to be brought together in syntheses.

In addition to archaeological excavations necessitated by new development, several Birmingham sites that could yield information of regional and national significance would benefit from large-scale, long-term and well-resourced excavations which include a full programme of analysis and publication.

PROTECTING THE PAST FROM MAN AND THE ELEMENTS

Archaeological remains surviving as buried features or earthworks, buildings or ruins above ground are vulnerable to damage from human activity or by water, weather, plants or animals. Protection from human damage is achieved by legal designation, through the planning process, and through increasing everyone's appreciation of the importance of these pieces of Birmingham's past.

Legal designation and the planning process

Some archaeological sites in Birmingham are designated Scheduled Monuments. These are sites that are considered to be nationally important and are protected by law. Some others, where the archaeological remains are structures above ground, are listed buildings and are similarly protected. Other sites are included in historic areas that are designated conservation areas and landscapes such as parkland whose importance is acknowledged through inclusion in a national register. All known archaeological sites and finds of all periods in Birmingham, including scheduled monuments and other sites which are of national importance, are recorded in the City Council's Historic Environment Record. Like every other local authority, the City Council has planning policies to protect archaeological remains that may be affected by new development. These are in line with government policy expressed in Planning Policy Statement 5, Planning for the Historic Environment. The City Council also has an Archaeology Strategy, which explains the policies and procedures in more detail.

Before it considers an application for planning permission for new development that is likely to affect archaeological remains, the City Council requires the applicant to submit an assessment of the significance of the archaeological remains and the likely effect of the development on them. This will consist of a desk-based assessment, which looks at all existing information about the site including any previous archaeological investigation and historic records, usually followed by an evaluation, which is a small-scale excavation to test what remains below ground. The desk-based assessment and archaeological evaluation are carried out by a professional archaeological organisation on behalf of the prospective developer. If the archaeological remains are of national importance, whether or not they are scheduled monuments, they must be preserved intact. This does not necessarily mean that no development can take place but that the foundations and layout of any new building must be arranged so that the archaeological remains are preserved. Even if the archaeological remains are not of national importance, they might still be preserved but if this is not feasible then they must be recorded before development starts, usually through archaeological excavation followed by analysis of the results and the publication of a detailed report. Like the desk-based assessment and archaeological evaluation, the archaeological excavation is carried out on the developer's behalf by a professional archaeological organisation. The cost of archaeological work necessitated by a development is met by the developer.

Publicising Birmingham's archaeology

There may also be a requirement as part of new development to display part of an archaeological site or to provide information to the public about it, as for example at Bullring in the city centre where display panels explain the results of the excavations that took place as part of the development.

The greatest threat to the survival of archaeological remains is ignorance of them. If owners or users of these sites, or visitors to them, are not aware of their existence and importance they will not be appreciated or understood and it is far more difficult to protect them. In Sutton Park, much of which is designated a scheduled monument, an archaeological interpretation scheme put together by two local groups consists of information panels, markers on

individual sites, a leaflet, an education pack and periodic guided walks. This has successfully increased visitors' awareness of well-preserved and nationally important archaeological remains *(99)*.

Protecting the past from the ravages of time

Archaeological remains are vulnerable to damage not only by new develop-ment but also through erosion by natural processes that inevitably occurs over time. One example shows how this can be controlled. As described in Chapter 2 above, most of Birmingham's burnt mounds are alongside streams and have been discovered as layers of heat-shattered stones and charcoal in the stream bank. The sites are visible because they are being eroded by the streams, but if this continued the sites would disappear completely. The burnt mound at Moseley Bog, a scheduled monument, has now been protected from stream erosion by the construction of a wattle work revetment along the stream bank *(100)*. A timber walkway set back from the bank replaces a path along the stream edge that was also causing damage to the site. Trees growing on the burnt mound have been felled to prevent damage through further root growth or through collapse of trees. The site is explained to visitors by an interpreta-tion panel attached to the sleeper walkway.

THE FUTURE

Bringing together the archaeological evidence for Birmingham's past demon-strates its contribution to our understanding of recent centuries as well as distant times. New discoveries and reconsideration of the results of archaeo-logical work that has already taken place will undoubtedly change some of our current perceptions of the hidden history revealed by archaeological remains. Additionally, opportunities arise to protect, incorporate and interpret archaeo-logical remains in new developments, making Birmingham's past part of the city's future.

Opposite
99 Marker near the Roman road in Sutton Park

100 Wattle revetment on the burnt mound at Moseley Bog

175

FURTHER READING

This is not a comprehensive list of all sources but is intended as a general guide to readily accessible publications. Much of the archaeological work whose results are included in this book has not yet been fully published, particularly that carried out over the past few years. However, summary reports appear in *West Midlands Archaeology* and information is included in the Historic Environment Record (see below).

West Midlands Archaeology (previously *West Midlands Archaeological News Sheet*) is produced annually by the Council for British Archaeology, West Midlands and contains short summaries of archaeological work carried out in that year.

Transactions of the Birmingham and Warwickshire Archaeological Society (previously *Transactions of the Birmingham Archaeological Society* and *Birmingham and Midland Institute, Archaeological Transactions*) is the main journal for publication of reports on archaeological work in Birmingham.

Copies of archaeological reports are deposited in Local Studies, Central Library, and Local Studies, Sutton Coldfield Library.

The Birmingham Historic Environment Record is the City Council's database of all known archaeological sites and finds in Birmingham. For further information see Birmingham City Council's archaeology website:
www.birmingham.gov.uk/archaeology

PUBLICATIONS ON BIRMINGHAM

British Association for the Advancement of Science, 1950 (reprint 1970) *Birmingham and its Regional Setting*: despite its age, this remains the best general introduction to the physical background.

Simon Buteux, 2003 *Beneath the Bull Ring*. Brewin: a summary of the results of the archaeological excavations of 1999-2001 in the historic heart of Birmingham.

William Hutton, various editions from 1782 *A History of Birmingham*.

Roger Lea, 2002 *The Story of Sutton Coldfield*. Sutton Publishing: a local history which incorporates some archaeological information.

Peter Leather, 2001 *A Brief History of Birmingham*. Brewin: brief but surprisingly comprehensive, and incorporating some archaeological information.

Peter Leather, 2002 *A Guide to the Buildings of Birmingham*. Tempus Publishing: a short but wide-ranging account which includes some archaeological sites.

Victor Skipp, 1970 *Medieval Yardley*. Phillimore: an excellent local history compiled from original documentary research, but without any information from archaeology

Chris Upton, 1993 *A History of Birmingham*. Phillimore: a general history which was written just before much of the recent archaeological work took place

Victoria County History: Warwickshire Volume VII covers the city of Birmingham as it was in the 1960s, Sutton Coldfield is in *Warwickshire Volume IV*, and King's Norton, Northfield and Yardley are in *Worcestershire Volume III*

SELECTED REPORTS ON BIRMINGHAM SITES

Prehistoric Birmingham and The Roman Empire and Beyond

Barfield, L. and Hodder, M., 'Burnt mounds in the West Midlands: Surveys and Excavations' in Gibson, A. (ed.) 1989 *Midlands Prehistory*. Oxford, British Archaeological Reports British Series, 204, 5-13

Jones, A., 2011, *Roman Birmingham 3: Excavations at Metchley Roman Forts 1999–2001 and 2004*, British Archaeological Reports British Series

Jones, A., Burrows, B., Evans, C.J., Hancocks, A., and Williams, J., 2008, *A Romano-British Livestock complex in Birmingham. Excavations 2002–2004 and 2006–2007 at Longdales Road, King's Norton, Birmingham*. British Archaeological Reports, British Series 471.

Powell, A.B., Booth, P., Fitzpatrick, A.P., and Crockett, A.D., and Fitzpatrick, A.P., 2008, *The Archaeology of the M6 Toll 2000–2003*. Oxford Wessex Archaeology Monograph 2

In *Transactions of the Birmingham and Warwickshire Archaeological Society* (volume, year and pages): Perry Barr pollen: 112, 2008, 1–11; Metchley Roman fort: 105, 2001 and 108, 2004; Rycknield Street: 60, 1936; Perry Barr pottery kiln: 77, 1959; Longbridge: 112, 2008, 45–72; various: 114, 2010

In *West Midlands Archaeology* (volume, year and pages): Banbury Street: 51, 2008, 86–88; Sutton Coldfield survey: 42, 1999; Northfield Relief Road: 49, 2006, 107; 121–2; Roman roads: 37, 1994; Wellhead Lane: 51, 2008, 104–5; Parsons Hill: 49, 2006, 105; Sutton Coldfield pottery kiln: 30, 1987

Medieval Birmingham and Into the Modern City

Patrick, C., and Ratkai, S., 2009, *The Bull Ring Uncovered; Excavations at Edgbaston Street, Moor Street, Park Street and The Row, Birmingham, 1997–2001*, Oxbow Books

Oswald, A., 1964, Excavation of a timber building at Weoley Castle, Birmingham, 1960–61, *Medieval Archaeology* 6–7, 109–134

Hislop, M., Demidowicz, G., and Price, S., 2011, 'Norteton . . . a praty uplandyshe towne': *Building recording, excavation and documentary research in King's Norton, Birmingham, 2005–2007*, British Archaeological Reports British Series

Brickley, M., Buteux, S., Adams, J. and Cherrington, R., 2007, *St Martin's Uncovered: Investigations in the churchyard of St Martin's-in-the-Bull-Ring, Birmingham, 2001*, Oxbow Books

Driver, L., Hislop, M., Litherland, S. and Ramsey, E., 2008, The north service range, Aston Hall, Birmingham: excavation and recording, 2004, *Post-Medieval Archaeology* 42/1, 104–129

In *Transactions of the Birmingham and Warwickshire Archaeological Society* (volume, year and pages): Birmingham Moat: 89, 1978–79, 1–77; Deritend: 73, 1957, 109–114; Coleshill Street, Sutton Coldfield: 109, 2005, 55–73; Kings Norton: 104, 2000, 101–121; Pool Hall: 50, 2007, 122; Hawkesley Farm: 76, 1958, 36–50; Kent's Moat: 82, 1967, 45–57; Weoley Castle: 78, 1962, 61–85; Selly Oak lime kilns: 109, 2005, 97–114; Edgbaston Mill: 111, 2007, 67–84; Hill Hook Mill: 93, 1983–84, 73–89; Longbridge: 112, 2008, 45–72; various: 114, 2010

In *West Midlands Archaeology* (volume, year and pages): Digbeth: 50, 2007, 103–104; Heath Mill Lane: 51, 2008, 88–89; Floodgate Street; 45, 2002, 106–108; Saracens Head: 49, 2006, 105–6; Minworth Greaves: 44, 2001, 193–194; Pool Hall: 50, 2007, 122; Primrose Hill Farm: 45, 2002, 113–114; Colmers Farm: 39, 1996, 100; High Street Bordesley: 48, 2005, 19–21; Cambridge Street: 52, 2010, 68; Lodge Road Glassworks: 51, 2008, 93–94; Belmont Glassworks and Ashted Engine: 50, 2007, 105–106; Soho Manufactory: 39, 1996, 20–24; Belmont Row decontamination unit: 51, 2008, 86–88

APPENDIX
WHAT YOU CAN SEE: SOME VISIBLE REMAINS OF BIRMINGHAM'S PAST

Birmingham Museum and Art Gallery's collections include prehistoric hand-axes, polished stone axes and bronze axes, Roman pottery from the Perry Barr kiln and from Parsons Hill, and medieval pottery, floor tiles and metalwork from Birmingham Moat, Weoley Castle and Kent's Moat. Soho House Museum, Soho Avenue, contains information about the Soho Manufactory and displays objects found in excavations there. Roman pottery from the Perry Barr kiln is on display in Handsworth Old Town Hall, Slack Lane.

The list below includes some of the more visible sites mentioned in this book. These are publicly accessible except for those marked ★, which are privately owned but are visible from adjoining public footpaths or roads and may be open to the public at times. Most of the sites in this list are scheduled monuments (SM). It is an offence to damage these sites in any way or to use a metal detector on them. Please help protect all of Birmingham's archaeological sites for the future.

PREHISTORIC BIRMINGHAM

Kings Standing Mound (SM): on open space alongside Kingstanding Road, north of junction with Cooksey Lane (SP 080955). A low mound with two trees on it.

Moseley Bog burnt mounds (SM): off Pensby Close/Yardley Wood Road (SP 093820). One of them is visible as a low mound next to a stream. There is an interpretation panel on a walkway near the site.

Burnt mounds in Sutton Park (SM): near Streetly Lane (SP 098987). One of the six mounds here is clearly visible. There is a marker on the site, which forms part of an archaeological interpretation scheme.

ROMAN BIRMINGHAM

Roman road in Sutton Park (SM): Runs near the western edge of Sutton Park. There are markers at two points on the road, near Chester Road North (Royal Oak Gate) (SP 084965) and near Thornhill Road (Streetly Gate) (SP 088985), which form part of an archaeological interpretation scheme.

Metchley Roman Fort (SM): off Vincent Drive, Edgbaston . There is a reconstructed corner of the defences (SP 041837) and part of the fort ditch is visible on the main University campus, with an interpretation panel between the access road and the canal (SP 044836).

Roman roads still in use: Icknield Street (SP 055777), Lifford Lane and part of Pershore Road (SP 054803) in Kings Norton follow the lines of a Roman road.

MEDIEVAL BIRMINGHAM

Edgbaston Street, Moor Street and Park Street: The results of excavations as part of the Bullring redevelopment are described on display panels in High Street, Edgbaston Street, and Moor Street in the Bullring.

Hawkesley Farm Moat (SM): Munslow Grove, Turves Green (SP 018776). Part of the moat, which now surrounds a tower block and bungalows, is now a pond and part is visible as a large dry ditch. There are two information panels on the site.

Kents Moat (SM): The Hays/Fleetwood Grove, off Sheldon Heath Road (SP 144862). The whole of the moat, now dry, survives and surrounds modern buildings.

Gannow Green Moat (SM): Devon Road (SO 984784). A well-preserved moat near the River Rea. There is a fishpond dam nearby, in Mull Close.

Sutton Park medieval fishponds (SM): Keepers, Wyndley and Bracebridge Pools are all medieval. Both the dam and quarry are particularly visible at Keepers Pool (SP 107965), where there is a marker as part of an archaeological interpretation scheme.

Ridge and furrow: Sheldon Country Park, near airport fence (SP 161854); Marion Way (SP 100813); Walkers Heath, east of Icknield Street★ (SP 056778).

Bromwich Wood boundary: off Scotland Lane (SO 999811).

Sutton Park deer park boundary (SM): The ditch and bank forming the outer boundary run along the present west and north sides of the park and have markers at points off Chester Road North (SP 085961) and off Streetly Lane (SP 094989) as part of an archaeological interpretation scheme. The subdividing banks and ditches can be seen near Keepers Pool where there is a marker on one of them.

Hollow ways: The former Yardley Green Road runs through Yardley Fields Recreation Ground (SP 127864).

POST–MEDIEVAL BIRMINGHAM

Edgbaston Street, Moor Street and Park Street: The results of excavations as part of the Bullring redevelopment are described on display panels in High Street, Edgbaston Street, and Moor Street.

Fox Hollies crucible pots★: off Fox Hollies Road (SP 147943). In a wall adjoining a public footpath.

Floodgate Street: Display panels in South Birmingham College★ describe the results of the excavations.

Fox Hill pottery kiln★: off Fox Hill Road (SP 139987). Visible from road

Woodgate Valley clay pits: off Clapgate Lane, in Woodgate Valley Country Park (SO 999830).

Barn Farm clay pit★: in field to north of Lindridge Road (SP 141970).

Belmont Glassworks★: off Lawley Middleway. Part of the boundary wall runs alongside the path from Lawley Middleway down to the canal (SP 080875).

Aston Flint Glassworks★: off Bagot Street. Part of the boundary wall is visible alongside the canal (SP 075880).

Sutton Park Old Peat Pit (SM): near Longmoor Brook opposite Rowtons Well (SP 092964).

Gas Street gasworks★: Gas Street (SP 062865). The outside of the renovated retort house is visible from the road.

Fazeley Street Gasworks★: off Fazeley Street (SP 081867). The retort house is visible from Fazeley Street and from the towpath of the adjoining canal.

Ashted Engine house: off Lawley Middleway, near Ashted Tunnel. The wall is visible from the towpath (SP 080875).

New Hall Mill★: off Wylde Green Road (SP 132945). The mill building is open to the public periodically, the headrace is visible from footpaths in New Hall Valley Country Park.

Sarehole Mill: Cole Bank Road (SP 099818). The tail race for Trittiford Mill and head and tail races for Sarehole Mill run alongside the River Cole from Coleside Avenue to Highfield Road and from Colebank Road to Green Road.

Moseley Bog: off Pensby Close (SP 094819). The dam of the now-drained millpool and a pond filling its quarry.

Sutton Park mill pools: Blackroot (SM), Longmoor (SM) and Powells Pools are all eighteenth-century mill pools. Blackroot and Longmoor have markers as part of an archaeological interpretation scheme and their dams and quarries are clearly visible.

Tame Valley Canal cutting: through Tower Hill and best viewed from Tower Hill footbridge (SP 055928).

Birmingham and Fazeley Canal embankment: off Cottage Lane and best viewed from Cottage Lane Bridge (SP 158924).

Lapal Tunnel Mounds: off Clapgate Lane, in Woodgate Valley Country Park (SO 998830)

Wasthill Tunnel mounds: off Shannon Road (SP 046776).

Blakesley Hall: Blakesley Road (SP 130862).

Sheldon Hall★: Gressel Lane (SP 162874). Now a public house.

Aston Hall and Park: Witton Lane (SP 079898).

Hamstead ice house and garden wall: in Garden Grove, off Greenway (SP 044926).

Hillwood Common enclosure landscape★: off Hillwood Common Road (SK 117005).

Hodge Hill Common mounds: off Coleshill Road (SP 133890).

Sutton Park wood boundaries and racecourse (SM): The enclosed woodland is mainly in the eastern half of the park, the racecourse is south-east of Blackroot Pool (SP 112967).

St Martin's churchyard (in the Bullring): The results of the excavations are explained on a display panel in St Martin's Square, to the north of the church.

Sutton Park targets (SM): off Chester Road North (SP 089966). There is a marker at the site as part of an archaeological interpretation scheme

Handsworth anti-aircraft gun installation: off Forge Lane (SP 034913). Approached from Forge Lane or car park for Hilltop golf course.

Harrisons Road wartime structure★: at junction of Harrisons Road and Richmond Hill Road (SP 045847).

Lifford pillbox★: off Pershore Road/Lifford Lane (SP 053080) Visible from towpath on opposite side of canal.

INDEX

If you are interested in purchasing other books published by The History Press,
or in case you have difficulty finding any of our books in your local bookshop,
you can also place orders directly through our website

www.thehistorypress.co.uk